PUPPET PLAYS PLUS

Hand Puppet Plays for Two Puppeteers

by
PHYLLIS NOE PFLOMM

The Scarecrow Press, Inc.
Metuchen, N.J., & London
1994

British Library Cataloguing-in-Publication data available

Library of Congress Cataloging-in-Publication Data

Pflomm, Phyllis Noe, 1925–
    Puppet plays plus : hand puppet plays for two puppeteers / by
Phyllis Noe Pflomm.
        p.   cm.
    ISBN 0-8108-2738-7 (acid-free paper)
    1. Puppet plays, American.   2. Puppet theater.   I. Title.
PN1980.P46   1994
812′.54—dc20   94-4875

Dedicated to my sons,
Elliot Richard Pflomm and
David Hayward Pflomm

.

TABLE OF CONTENTS

ACKNOWLEDGMENTS

Special thanks to Charlotte Leonard, retired Coordinator of Children's Services (Dayton & Montgomery County Public Library), for her help in preparing this manuscript for publication and for providing information regarding the development of the DMCPL puppet program. I also thank Jeri Kladder, formerly "the puppeteer on the left" and now with the Public Library of Columbus & Franklin County, for her encouragement at the onset of this project; friend Rita Ollech for suggestions about the audience participation plays; Silvana Leone, my coworker at the Ft. McKinley Branch Library, for supplying several ideas for plays; Jennie Eisnaugle, Children's Librarian of the Northmont Branch Library, for taking the photographs; and others in the DMCPL system: Tish Wilson, Coordinator of Children's Services; Derrick Stiles and Scott Hawkins (Audio Visual Department); and lastly, the members of Chairperson Jennie Eisnaugle's Puppet Committee, whose talent has brought my plays to life: Jan Becker, Cindy Butcher, Teresa Low, and especially Julia Gilbert, who arranged for professional tapings.

INTRODUCTION

Since the early seventies, puppet shows have been a regular part of the programming for juvenile patrons of the Dayton & Montgomery County Public Library where I work. There are two theaters, the Peppermint Palace for marionettes and the Lollipop Puppet Theater for hand puppet shows.

As children's librarian at the Ft. McKinley Branch Library, I was eager to try my hand at puppetry. I thought marionettes would be lots of fun, so I arranged to borrow the portable stage that is shared by all of the libraries in the system. Working together, Jeri Kladder, children's librarian at the nearby Dayton View Branch, and I managed to put it together. Once assembled, this ingeniously designed stage looked magnificent. It also took about half the floor space in the children's section. But my partner and I were committed—two days of shows at my branch and two days at hers.

Good planners, we had, of course, allowed time for practice. That a two-hour rehearsal is not nearly enough for rank amateurs to master marionettes was soon apparent. Somehow, Jeri and I survived, and the children who saw those shows are grown and have no doubt forgotten, but I will always remember the missed entrances, the twisted strings, and the puppets, either dangling inches above the stage floor or collapsed in a heap.

I learned from that experience that it is virtually impossible to keep an eye on a script and manipulate marionettes at the same time. Even a pretaped play (which ours are) has directions that are in no way indicated by the recording. Therefore, complete familiarity with the script is essential, plus more hours of rehearsal time than most children's librarians could ever manage. So it was good-bye forever to marionettes.

Besides comparative ease in manipulation, there was another good reason to turn to hand puppets. Each branch in the library system has its own hand puppet stage, which can be set up in minutes. The time saved can better be spent rehearsing. Even though a show is taped and hand puppets are relatively easy to use, rehearsal is still a must. But, at least with hand puppets, two or three run-throughs will usually suffice to ensure a satisfactory result.

One problem has always been that our scripts have not included any production notes. Therefore, a certain amount of time was always frittered away deciding which puppets to assign to each puppeteer, which side to use for each entrance and exit, etc. That is why, when I began writing these plays for hand puppets, I decided to include specific stage directions. The production notes following each piece are not written in stone. They should be regarded as suggestions, many of which—especially since puppet stages vary—may well be improved upon. Perhaps the hints will most benefit those of you who may be using hand puppets for the first time. Others may view them as a jumping-off point.

Most of the pieces require two puppeteers. I have designated their positions as left and right, and as I wrote, I described the action from the puppeteer's point of view backstage. This is really unimportant, since the action described would work just as well from the audience viewpoint, as long as it remains consistent. For some reason I have always been the puppeteer on the right.

The switch to using hand puppets did not mean that everything has gone perfectly ever after. Timing is still occasionally off; props are sometimes mishandled or dropped; once a puppet's head even fell off into the audience. Such are the pitfalls of live entertainment, and the children—bless them—are tolerant. They have not come to the library expecting to see the Muppets, and they seem to enjoy the intimacy that a live performance offers.

The shows in this book are meant for children from about three to eight years old. They were written to be used by amateur puppeteers—librarians, teachers, and other nonprofessional groups, children as well as adults. The project has been a satisfying one for me, and I hope that the final product will be useful and also fun—for both audience and puppeteers.

Phyllis Noe Pflomm

PUPPETS IN HISTORY

Puppetry predates written history. In various forms, puppets have long figured in the lives of people almost everywhere in the world. There is evidence of articulated dolls being used ceremonially in ancient Egypt, India, and Greece. Independent of old-world influence, native Americans created their own kinds of puppets for ritual use.

In Europe much early puppet theater, like other drama, was religiously oriented. Classical legends and folklore also provided themes for the plays. Both marionettes and hand puppets were used in Europe, and traveling shows were popular. A single puppeteer touring on foot could literally carry a hand puppet theater to his audience. By the eighteenth century some established marionette shows were quite elaborate, even featuring specially written opera music by the most respected composers. Performances, for the most part, were considered adult entertainment.

The word puppet is derived from the Latin *pupa*, which means doll. There are four main kinds: hand puppets, marionettes, rod puppets, and shadow puppets.

Hand puppets are sometimes called glove puppets because of the way they fit the puppeteer's hand. Head and arms are moved by the user's thumb and fingers. Another type is constructed to move its mouth instead. Hand puppets are operated from below. Although he evolved from an Italian marionette, Punch, the violent hero of the Punch-and-Judy shows, is a famous example of a hand puppet.

Marionettes are sometimes called string puppets. They are jointed dolls manipulated from above by strings or wires. In Collodi's classic *Pinocchio*, the little protagonist is a marionette.

Rod puppets are operated by sticks, usually from below stage. A central rod is inserted into the puppet's head, and jointed arms are moved by secondary rods. The four-foot Bunraku puppets of Japan are rod puppets operated from behind.

Shadow puppets are flat, jointed figures operated from below by rods or sticks. Lit from behind, their silhouettes are projected on a cloth screen. Shadow puppets, usually of intricate design, have long been popular in China and Indonesia. Shadow plays have also been attractions at country fairs in America.

Other puppets are composite. For example, the Muppets, today's beloved television stars, are mixed-style, hand-rod puppets. Their mouths are hand operated, and their arms are moved with rods.

At its best, puppetry is a highly developed art form, sometimes requiring lifelong commitment of its practitioners. The puppets used by these professionals are often works of art, befitting the skills of those who use them. Marionettes, rod, and shadow puppets generally are more complicated than hand puppets and would be more likely to fall into this category.

Conversely, hand puppets can be used successfully by almost anyone, which is why they are favored by most nonprofessionals. Even though today's children are exposed to top-notch productions on television, there is nothing like experiencing the real thing. So live puppet shows, most of which are put on by amateur groups, continue to delight the children who see them.

PLANNING THE PROGRAM

Audience age should be the first consideration when planning a puppet program. The plays in this book are for children from about three to eight years old. With the exception of the two-part audience participation piece, "Let's Be Puppets," none lasts longer than fifteen minutes.

If the group is made up exclusively of preschoolers, the program should not exceed half an hour, and a break in the middle is a good idea. "Exercise Time," lead by Missy Muscle, would work well as a break. So would a song or dance in which the kids can participate. Children from kindergarten to third grade will enjoy

Children enjoy meeting the puppets after a show.

5

Neighborhood children enjoy a puppet show at the Northmont Branch Library in Englewood, Ohio.

a slightly longer program. Some of the plays are geared to this older group.

When pieces are being considered, their exact playing time (including introductory music) should be calculated. After two or three are selected, the program can be rounded out to the desired length. Songs, dances, and poems make good fillers. Another idea, especially near a patriotic holiday, would be a parade. To the accompaniment of band music, all of the puppets can pass by (perhaps more than once) carrying a variety of flags, banners, bells, etc.

PUPPETS

With several exceptions all of the puppets in the following plays should be hand (glove) puppets. There are two kinds that may be designated as such. In this book they are called *hand-action* if their arms and heads are manipulated and *mouth-action* if their mouths move. What the puppet is required to do determines what kind it should be. A mix of hand and mouth-action puppets is acceptable and often works best. The production notes following each play specify what style of puppets the characters should be.

HAND-ACTION PUPPETS: People puppets should usually be hand-action because they are often required to manipulate props. If a puppet is supposed to be a person, logic dictates that it would normally hold or carry props in its hands. If a puppet lacking maneuverable hands should suddenly seize a prop in its mouth while continuing to talk, the play would immediately lose credibility, and any laughter that results would be for the wrong reason. Even puppet plays must be believable, so whenever the stage directions indicate the use of props by a puppet in the role of a person, the hand-action variety is in order. Some animals have manual dexterity, so a raccoon or monkey could also logically be hand-action.

MOUTH-ACTION PUPPETS: Generally, animal puppets work best if they are mouth-action. They can then talk, sing, laugh, or make animal noises, and if the action requires them to carry props, using the mouth to do so would seem right. People puppets that do nothing but talk are also most effective if they are mouth-action. The loquacious Ms. Potts in "The Talent Show" is an example. Simple mouth-action puppets made from socks or soft felt are easily manipulated and can be made to assume a variety of facial expressions.

Hand puppets by their nature never have legs, although legs are sometimes added as decorative appendages. Likewise, arms can be attached to the side seams of a mouth-action puppet if much of the body is visible. Puppets that fit the hand too tightly inhibit action.

7

If they are too loose, they are difficult to keep on. A hand-action puppet should cover the hand like a large glove, the thumb and third finger inserted into the puppet's arms and the forefinger into its head. The neckpiece should fit snugly. A mouth-action puppet should fit the hand like a mitten, the thumb operating the lower jaw and the fingers the upper jaw.

The two simple patterns included here should be regarded as a starting point for beginners who want to try their hands at making puppets. There are many excellent books on the subject, some of which are included in a reading list at the end of this book. There is also a list of suggestions about where to buy ready-made puppets.

HAND-ACTION PUPPET
(BASIC PATTERN)

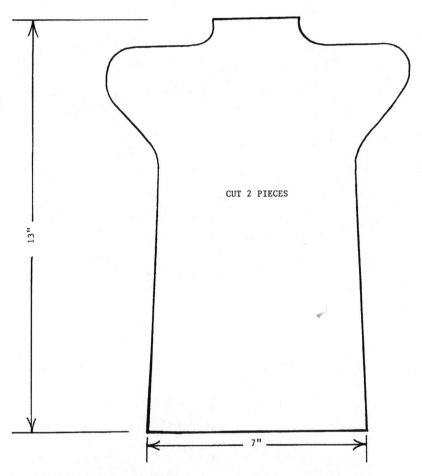

CUT 2 PIECES

13"

7"

Stitch body sides together. Use a foam ball for the head. After cutting a hole for the forefinger, insert a neck of rolled cardboard. Glue this to the costume neck, and add appropriate features to the face.
(Papier-mâché or stuffed cloth heads may also be used)

MOUTH-ACTION PUPPET
(BASIC PATTERN)

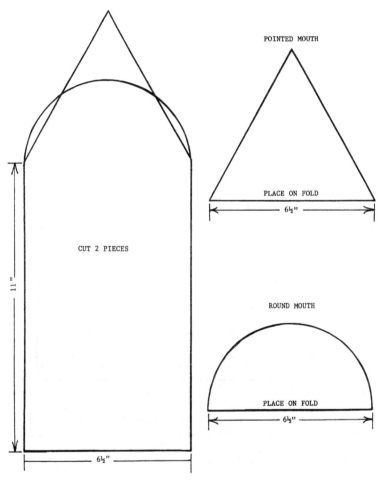

POINTED MOUTH

PLACE ON FOLD

6½"

CUT 2 PIECES

11"

ROUND MOUTH

PLACE ON FOLD

6½"

6½"

Stitch body sides together and sew in the mouth. Decorate with appropriate features.

STAGE SETUP

STAGE: A hand puppet stage can take many forms. It can be as simple as a standing screen that hides the puppeteers from view. One popular style that works well and takes little storage space is a basic frame stage on platform feet. The opening is covered by a black scrim backdrop against which the drama is viewed by the audience. This material is sheer enough for the puppeteers to observe the action from behind. For a more finished look, front curtains may be hung around the opening.

In a scene from "The Picnic" the raccoon discovers the picnic basket. A temporary prop made from a shoe box lid is covered with construction paper.

*Each branch of the Dayton and Montgomery County Public Library system has a
simple frame puppet stage (39 inches wide by 48 inches high). Here the stage has been
mounted on a cloth covered bench. The black scrim backdrop is in place, and the
brackets for the front curtain rods are visible.*

PROP STAGE: Some plays require props to be set down, so some
kind of prop stage is necessary. The ideal puppet stage would have a
permanent prop stage, i.e. a proscenium ledge or shelf several inches
wide extending the length of the frame opening. Lacking this, a shoe
box lid can be covered in construction paper and cut to fit across the
frame.

SETTINGS: Scenery should not be used in amateur hand puppet
plays. The puppeteers will already (literally) have their hands full
managing puppets and props, so the simpler the settings, the better.
Usually dialogue, action, and portable props are enough to suggest a
setting. Using permanent props for specific scenes should be done
only when the action demands.

PROPS: Coming up with the right prop is often a matter of luck.
Toy stores are sometimes the answer, since all sorts of accessories are
made for dolls. Props need not be perfectly scaled to a puppet's size.

Setup behind the scenes at the Ft. McKinley Branch Library.

In fact, something proportionately a bit too large will be more visible to the audience. When all else fails, props must be made. Construction paper, Play-Doh™, miscellaneous craft supplies, and just plain junk can be turned into all manner of interesting objects.

TAPE PLAYER: Once the stage is in place, the tape player must be positioned for easy accessibility by both puppeteers. The tapes should be placed nearby in proper order. If the tape player has stereo speakers with long cords, the speakers should be pulled forward beside the stage.

SCRIPTS: Scripts should be typed single-spaced (double-spaced between speeches) and taped to the puppet stage or the rod of the scrim curtain for easy referral by the puppeteers.

MUSIC

MUSIC helps to set the mood for a puppet play. It can be popular or classical as long as the sound suits the subject. Usually instrumental music works best. Surprisingly, the faster-paced movements of symphonies (allegretto, allegro, or presto) are often good choices. Other possibilities include piano or guitar music or even something played on a toy xylophone, bells, or kazoo.

In lieu of music, appropriate sound effects could be used. For example, ghostly moans and rattling chains would provide a fitting introduction to a Halloween play. Whatever is chosen to introduce a play should not last much longer than 30 seconds or the attention of the audience will wane. Then the volume should decrease, fading out completely as the play begins. This is easy to manage if a record or cassette is used.

SONGS can be used effectively at the beginning or end of a program or between plays. Children enjoy singing along with the puppets, if they know the words, and clapping in time to the music. *Sesame Street* songs are much enjoyed, and *Rudolph, the Red-nosed Reindeer* and *Frosty the Snowman* are big hits in December programs.

For amateur productions there should be no problem using commercially made records or tapes. If the program is to be a money-making enterprise, however, permission should be obtained from the record company.

TAPING

In the past, puppet plays were memorized, and puppeteers spoke as they manipulated their puppets. Of course, this can still be done, but it is no longer necessary. Taping on a cassette recorder is suggested as the best way to ensure a successful production. The finest available recording equipment should be used, but even a simple recorder can produce satisfactory results. Using high-quality tape is more important.

VOICES: It is important that the actors' voices differ from one another, especially in long dialogues. Voices can vary in cadence, speed, texture, and especially pitch. Small puppet characters (children or tiny animals) should generally have high voices. The voice of a character of authority should usually be lower and/or louder. This will seem logical to the audience, and the distinctions will also help the puppeteers who must later manipulate the puppets according to the sound. As much appropriate emotion as possible should be instilled into the speeches as the script is read.

SOUND EFFECTS: Some plays require special sound effects. Any equipment needed to produce these effects should be handy during recording so that the sounds can be put on the tape. Specific suggestions about achieving the sounds are included in the production notes following the plays.

TIMING: The most convincing recording counts for nothing if pauses are not properly observed. For example, if a character is supposed to exit to get a prop and then reenter, several seconds must be allowed or the moves that the puppeteer must later make will trail behind the sound. In these plays ellipses (. . .) have been used to indicate pauses in the sound. These vary in time, and common sense should dictate the length of each pause. Stage directions also occasionally indicate that there should be a pause in the recording.

REHEARSING: To produce a good tape, rehearsal is essential. Several run-throughs are suggested, complete with sound effects.

RECORDING: Once the above preliminaries have been observed, it is time to tape. Someone familiar with the play should act as director and follow the script during recording. If one of the actors muffs a line, or a vital pause is not observed, the tape can be stopped and the mistake corrected. The end product should be a high-quality recording that can be used many times.

PLAYING TIME: The tape, including any music or special sound effects used before or during the play, should be timed exactly. The times included in the production notes of the following plays are approximate.

ACTION

Most of these plays require two puppeteers. Even the pieces with only two characters will work best with an extra person behind the scenes. After a puppet is onstage for several minutes, its operator will be grateful to have a spare hand as an elbow prop beneath an upraised arm. The backstage operators have been designated here as *The Puppeteer on the Right* and *The Puppeteer on the Left,* and specific production notes indicate what each should do in the plays. Right and left are considered from the puppeteers' point of view.

Scene from "The Valentine Bouquet." The puppet on the left has a styrofoam ball head topped with yellow yarn hair. A small, flexible hand-action puppet like this can assume many roles.

17

REHEARSAL: While having a play on tape frees puppeteers from memorizing or reading aloud during the production, some rehearsal is essential. Enough time should be allowed for the puppeteers to feel confident in their ability to synchronize movement to sound while keeping one eye on the handily posted script. The final run-through should be a dress rehearsal with everything set up as if for an actual performance. Puppets and props should be arranged in order. Some elegant stages have shelves or hooks for easy accessibility, but lacking this, a book truck or bench behind the puppeteers works well.

ENTRANCES AND EXITS: Unless indicated otherwise, puppets should not pop up from below. They should enter in profile position as a real person or animal would, maintaining a consistent onstage level. They should exit the same way.

HAND-ACTION PUPPETS: If a puppet is a person, the puppeteer should keep his/her hand in a vertical position unless the script indicates otherwise. While talking, the puppet's arms and head should move. Listening, the puppet should be motionless. In conversation, puppets should turn slightly toward one another. If a

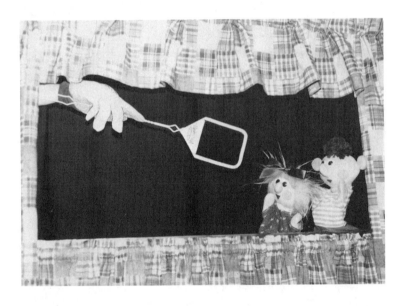

Bryan and Susie meet the Flyswatter in "Litterbugs."

hand-action puppet is an animal, it may be held in a forward position.

MOUTH-ACTION PUPPETS: If the puppet is a person, the puppeteer's arm should be vertical, elbow to wrist, and the hand bent forward at a right angle. Animal puppets can assume a more relaxed position, inclining forward, especially if addressing the audience. A puppet's mouth should not wobble constantly while talking or singing, but should open on stressed vowels.

EMOTING: A puppet, though small, can be made to exhibit larger-than-life emotions. Happy, it can jump, dance, and (if hand-action) clap its hands in glee. Called upon to cry, a puppet can throw itself down and thrash violently, much to the enjoyment of the audience. Mouth-action puppets, especially the soft homemade variety, can be made to portray a wide gamut of emotions. Puppets should be made to "ham it up" whenever the script allows.

THE VALENTINE BOUQUET

PUPPETS

MOLLY
CHIP
CORKY
DAISY
MOTHER

PROPS

PAPER HEART
PILL BOTTLE VASE
5 LOLLIPOPS
DOLL

MOLLY: (*enters with paper heart . . . addresses audience*) This is a valentine I made in school today. I really love to make valentines. It's so easy to do. All you need is a piece of paper folded in the middle and some scissors. Then you cut a smooth, careful curve, up, over, and down. When you open it up, you have a heart like this. . . . You can make little hearts or big hearts, skinny hearts or fat hearts. This one is big *and* fat, because it's for my mother. I wanted room for plenty of hugs and kisses. See? (*shows valentine*) The Os are hugs, and the Xs are kisses. . . . But this Valentine's Day, I'm giving my mother a present, too, because I have something this year that I don't usually have—money! (*crosses stage*) I'm going in the house to get my money now, but first I'll tape this valentine to the refrigerator door where Mom will find it. The present—that'll be the real surprise—will come later. (*exits with heart . . . enters*) And now I'm off to the Candy Corner to buy something special. (*crosses stage and exits . . . enters with vase of lollipops*) . . . How about this for a valentine gift? And, let me tell you, these are not ordinary lollipops. They are chocolate. So this is a valentine bouquet of milk chocolate pops. I can hardly wait to give it to Mom. (*starts across stage . . . stops*) I know what I'll do! Instead of taking this inside, I'll ring the doorbell and say, "Special delivery for Valentine's Day." That will make the surprise even better.

CHIP: (*enters*) Hey, Molly, wait up.

MOLLY: Oh, hi, Chip.

CHIP: What's that you have?

MOLLY: It's a present for my mother for Valentine's Day.

CHIP: A bunch of lollipops? That's weird.

MOLLY: What do you mean, weird? This is a *bouquet* of lollipops, and they're not just any old kind either. They're milk chocolate pops. That's very, very special.

CHIP: Yum, yum, that does sound special. I sure wish I had something like that for my mother.

MOLLY: Uh-huh.

CHIP: Yes, I'd really like to give my Mom a nice present like that.

MOLLY: Uh-huh.

CHIP: My mom really loves chocolate.

MOLLY: Uh-huh.

CHIP: (*sadly*) Yes, even just one milk chocolate pop would be a nice surprise for my mom.

MOLLY: Well, Chip, they have lots of these left at the Candy Corner.

CHIP: Uh-huh.

MOLLY: Is there any reason why you can't go down there yourself and buy a milk chocolate pop?

CHIP: Uh-huh. The best reason in the world.

MOLLY: Oh, I know why. You don't have any money.

CHIP:	You are a very smart person, Molly, besides being my best friend.
MOLLY:	Why, thank you.
CHIP:	You are very, very smart.
MOLLY:	Uh-huh.
CHIP:	And my very, very, very best friend.
MOLLY:	(*angrily*) All right. All right. Don't say I can't take a hint. Here, take one of mine. (*He takes a pop*)
CHIP:	Thank you, thank you, thank you. You're a really-truly friend.
MOLLY:	You're welcome. I think I'm a really-truly sucker, and I don't mean a lollipop. Well, never mind. Wish your mom a happy Valentine's Day for me.
CHIP:	I will. Thanks again, Molly. Good-bye. (*exits*)
MOLLY:	Well, I have four milk chocolate pops left, and that's still a nice present. . . . (*loud crying offstage*) . . . My goodness, who's that?
CORKY:	(*enters sobbing*) Waahh. . . . Waahh. . . .
MOLLY:	Why, Corky, what's the matter? Why are you crying?
CORKY:	I . . . I . . . I fell down in the mud.
MOLLY:	I can see that. Are you hurt?
CORKY:	No, but look at my clothes. I'm covered with slick, slimy, sloppy mud. (*sobs*)
MOLLY:	Yes, you are a mess. But, don't worry, the dirt will come out in the wash.
CORKY:	But I'm staying at my grandma's, and she'll be mad at me.
MOLLY:	Your grandma is a nice lady. She won't be mad at you.

CORKY: Oh, yes, she will. She'll punish me. Oh, I'm going to get it, something awful.

MOLLY: But it was an accident. You didn't fall down on purpose, did you?

CORKY: No, but Grandma told me to stay inside and keep clean, because we're going out later.

MOLLY: But you went outside anyway.

CORKY: Yes. And now Grandma will be mad at me, won't she?

MOLLY: Yes, I think your grandma will be mad all right.

CORKY: Very, very mad?

MOLLY: Yes, and I don't blame her.

CORKY: So that's why I'm crying. (*sobs*)

MOLLY: Poor little Corky. You were naughty, that's for sure. But I can't help feeling sorry for you. . . . Say, I have an idea. I'll give you one of these milk chocolate pops. You can give it to your grandma and say, "Happy Valentine's Day."

CORKY: Oh, goody! Then she won't be mad, will she?

MOLLY: I don't know. Maybe not *quite* so mad. Here you are. Take one of these for your grandma.

CORKY: (*takes a pop*) Thank you, Molly. I'll give it to her right now. (exits)

MOLLY: (*calls after Corky*) Be sure to give her a big hug, too. . . . My bouquet is getting smaller. But three milk chocolate pops are still a pretty nice present. . . . (*loud crying offstage*) . . . I can't believe it. Here comes another unhappy person. . . . Why, it's Daisy.

DAISY: (*enters sobbing with doll*) Waahhh. . . . Waahhh. . . .

MOLLY: Daisy, what's the matter? You didn't fall down in the mud, did you?

DAISY: No. (*sobs*)

MOLLY: Something must be wrong. Why are you crying?

DAISY: It's . . . it's . . . it's my dolly. . . . Look. (*shows doll*)

MOLLY: (*looks*) Oh, now I see. . . . Your doll has lost a leg.

DAISY: Yes. Oh, my poor dolly! (*sobs*)

MOLLY: Maybe we can find it.

DAISY: No, it fell down a hole in the street. (*sobs*)

MOLLY: Oh, I'm sorry. Is there anything I can do to make you feel better?

DAISY: No. The only thing that ever makes me feel better when I'm unhappy is candy. (*sobs*)

MOLLY: I might have guessed that candy would be the answer to your problem. But now *I* have a problem. . . . Daisy, if I give you a delicious milk chocolate pop, would that make you feel better?

DAISY: (*laughs*) Oh, yes!

MOLLY: Well, all right. Here you are then.

DAISY: Oh, happy day! Good-bye, stupid doll. (*flings doll away*) Hello, yummy milk chocolate pop! (*grabs pop and exits*)

MOLLY: (*addresses audience*) I can't believe it. She just threw her doll away. . . . This day isn't turning out the way it was supposed to. I started out with a bouquet of milk chocolate pops, and now only two are left. I'd better hurry home before I meet any more unhappy people. (*crosses stage*) Now I'm the unhappy one. But I'll ring the doorbell anyway, as planned. (*puts down vase and rings doorbell*)

MOTHER: (*enters*) Why, Molly!

MOLLY: (*sadly*) Special delivery for Valentine's Day.

MOTHER: (*picks up vase*) Oh, how lovely! A valentine present for me.

MOLLY: Not a very nice present.

MOTHER: Whatever do you mean? I think it's perfect. I'll put it inside. (*deposits vase offstage*)

MOLLY: When I left the Candy Corner I had a bouquet of milk chocolate pops, and now two are all I have left for you. I wish I hadn't met three unhappy people on my way home, but I did, and I gave away part of your present.

MOTHER: But you made three people happy by sharing.

MOLLY: I guess so.

MOTHER: I'm glad there are exactly two left. Can you guess why?

MOLLY: No, why?

MOTHER: Because I know you like chocolate, too, so we'll have a Valentine's Day party. For dessert there will be one pop for me and one for you. Won't that be nice?

MOLLY: I guess so.

MOTHER: But I found something even nicer earlier today.

MOLLY: What's that?

MOTHER: A valentine on the refrigerator door.

MOLLY: But that's just a paper heart I cut out.

MOTHER: But it's covered with Os and Xs. I do like chocolate, but hugs and kisses are even better. . . . (*They hug*) . . .

MOLLY: Happy Valentine's Day, Mom.

MOTHER: Happy Valentine's Day, Molly. Now let's go have our party. (*They exit*)

The Valentine Bouquet

PUPPETS: All of the puppets should be hand-action. Molly must be very flexible because she is required to hold the pill bottle for most of the play. Corky and Daisy should be small, designating that they are the youngest characters, and Corky's clothing should show signs of mud.

SETTING: All of the action takes place outside. A prop stage is needed briefly when Molly puts down the vase, which she must do before ringing the doorbell.

PROPS: The paper heart should have a noticeable fold and be about five inches so that the audience can see the Xs and Os. A cylindrical pharmacy pill container (2 1/2″ high by 1 3/4″ in diameter) is perfect for the vase. Five Tootsie Roll™ Pops fit this exactly, but the candy should be replaced by something lightweight such as cotton or paper balls, which can be covered in foil. The doll could be a small rubber (or plastic) one or a simple cloth one with a missing leg. It should not be made of anything breakable.

TAPING: The only special effect is the sound of the doorbell, which could be a chime of some kind or sounds made by a toy piano or xylophone. Molly's voice must contrast decidedly with those of the other characters with whom she converses in sequence.

ACTION: The puppeteer on the left should be Molly and her mother, and the one on the right should operate the tape player and be the other three characters.

Molly first enters from the right with the heart, talks, and then crosses stage, exiting and reentering from the left (her home). Then she crosses stage and exits right (the Candy Corner), reentering with the lollipop bouquet. She stays holding the vase at center stage, and Chip, Corky, and Daisy enter and exit at the right. When Daisy flings her doll away, she merely drops it backstage. The mother enters from the left and stays at far left stage (the door to her home). Molly must put the vase down briefly in order to ring the doorbell and also because it will be easier for her mother to pick it up from the prop stage than for one puppet to hand it to the other. The mother deposits it offstage (the puppeteer's free hand) so that the puppets can hug.

TIME: 10 minutes. Allow extra time for introductory music.

THE LEPRECHAUN

CHARACTERS

LEPRECHAUN
PIG
3 LEPRECHAUNS

PROP

SHOE

	(*sound of pounding offstage* . . . *tap* . . . *tap* . . . *tap* . . . *tap, tap, tap, tap, tap, tap, tap, tap* . . . *tap* . . . *tap* . . . *tap* . . . *tap* . . . *loud clunk as something heavy hits floor*)
LEPRECHAUN:	(*enters with shoe*) Oh, shame on me! I've been a shoemaker all my blessed life, and I've never, never, never thrown my hammer before. . . . But I'm tired of making shoes. . . . Tired, tired, tired. (*looks at shoe*) Ahhh, this is a pretty one. The stitching is perfect, if I say so myself, and the sole is tender to the foot, soft, but not too soft. . . . Yes, this shoe is my masterpiece, the best, the very best, I've ever made. . . . All it needed was one more nail. . . . But I'm sick of making shoes. Sick, sick, sick. So, pretty shoe, away you go! (*throws shoe*) Oh, I feel better already. I should have done this long ago.
PIG:	(*enters*) Hey, somebody threw a shoe, and it knocked me on the noggin.
LEPRECHAUN:	Saints preserve me! It's a talking pig.
PIG:	That I am. And I just got a nasty bump on my head.
LEPRECHAUN:	Oh, dearie me. I'm afraid that I'm the guilty

	party. The shoe just slipped from my hand, and through the air it flew.
PIG:	Well, I hope from now on you'll be more careful.
LEPRECHAUN:	That I will, to be sure. And, really, I am very sorry. I hope that the knock on your noggin was not too painful.
PIG:	I accept your apology. And, to tell the truth, it didn't hurt all that much. It was a rather small shoe. It was a very, very small shoe, in fact.
LEPRECHAUN:	Yes, but never mind about that. I'm glad you weren't hurt, so good-bye.
PIG:	Not so fast, sir. I think, since I am the one who suffered the injury, that I deserve to have my curiosity satisfied. It's the least you can do.
LEPRECHAUN:	Hah! This talking pig wants his curiosity satisfied. And he speaks like a scholar. . . . Very well, Mr. Pig, what do you want to know?
PIG:	I would like to know how you came by this tiny shoe. It is far too small for any human being I know. Paddy, whose pig I am proud to be, has a great, broad foot. Even his baby could not wear so small a shoe.
LEPRECHAUN:	Ah, so you are Paddy's pig! I might have known, since he and his vast brood live just down the lane. . . . Well, Pig, to answer your question, or, as you would say, satisfy your curiosity, I did not merely come by that shoe, as you put it. I made it. But I do not make shoes for the likes of Paddy. I make shoes only for the wee folk.
PIG:	The wee folk! Do you mean fairies?
LEPRECHAUN:	That I do. That I do. It's my job—I might even be so bold as to say *career*—to make shoes for fairies. I am known as the best fairy shoemaker in this part of Ireland.
PIG:	Then you must be a leprechaun!

LEPRECHAUN: That I am. That I am.

PIG: This is exciting. I've heard about leprechauns, but I never thought I'd meet one.

LEPRECHAUN: Well, now you have. So, good-bye.

PIG: Oh, you shan't be rid of me yet. My curiosity is still not completely satisfied, and you owe me that. . . . Why, I'd like to know, did that shoe come sailing through the air to hit me on my noggin? I don't believe for a minute that it merely slipped from your hand.

LEPRECHAUN: All right, I'll admit it. I threw the shoe, but I didn't mean to hit anyone. If truth be known, I'm a bit bored. Day and night, night and day, I stitch and pound, making shoes. Work, work, work, that's all I ever do. It's those dancing fairies who have all the fun. While I work, they dance and wear out the shoes I've made for them. And when the soles are thin and the stitching frayed, they come back for repairs.

PIG: But surely they pay you for your work.

LEPRECHAUN: Oh, yes. They bring gold, lots of beautiful gold. I am very, very rich.

PIG: Then it's true what they say. I've heard that every leprechaun has a pot of gold buried somewhere.

LEPRECHAUN: Yes, that's true. And now I know what you're after. You want my pot of gold. Well, I'm not going to tell you where it is.

PIG: Hah! Now, I ask you, what would a pig want with gold? I have no need for fine clothes or other fancy things. And I certainly wouldn't go to market to buy a pound of pork chops. Ugh, what a horrible thought!

LEPRECHAUN: So, at last it's good-bye.

PIG: Not quite yet. I have an idea. Why don't you have a leprechauns' dance? There must be others of your kind about.

LEPRECHAUN: Oh, yes. Leprechauns live in hollow trees and under stumps all around here, but we never get together. Leprechauns are loners. . . . But just once, dancing a bit might be fun.

PIG: Then leave it to me. Now that I know where to look I'm going to see if I can find some more leprechauns like yourself who might enjoy kicking up their heels. So, *now* it's good-bye. (*exits*)

LEPRECHAUN: Good-bye to you too. . . . Humph! I'm sure that pig means well, but I don't think there's going to be any leprechauns' dance. . . . Well, I guess I've had my tantrum. Now I'd best look for that shoe I tossed away and get back to work. (*searches*) Where is it? I'm sure I didn't throw it far. . . . Ah, good! Here it is. (*picks up shoe*) And now, It's back to work for me. (*exits with shoe . . . sound of pounding offstage . . . tap . . . tap . . . tap . . . tap . . . tap*)

PIG: (*enters*) Mr. Leprechaun, Mr. Leprechaun, where are you? I bring news, and 'tis fitting for the season.

LEPRECHAUN: (*enters*) Oh, it's the talking pig again. Whatever do you mean? What news do you bring?

PIG: The best. The leprechauns' dance is arranged, and just in time for St. Patrick's Day, too. 'Twill begin shortly.

LEPRECHAUN: You don't say.

PIG: Yes, I discovered some others like you who were fed up with working. . . . The music is about to begin, so follow me. (*exits followed by leprechaun . . . they re-enter from opposite side*)

LEPRECHAUN: (*looking about*) Where are all the others?

PIG: Oh, they'll be along, never fear. And now, since I've done my good deed, I'll be running along. I hope you will enjoy your dance and have a happy St. Patrick's Day as well.

LEPRECHAUN: Thank you, Mr. Pig, and the same to you. (*The music begins, and the leprechaun begins to dance alone. One by one, three others enter, and they dance solemnly in unison. . . . As the music fades, the leprechauns exit, one by one in single file, still dancing.*)

The Leprechaun

PUPPETS: The four leprechauns should be hand-action pup-
            pets. Although, according to some scholarly
            sources, leprechauns traditionally wore red jack-
            ets, green, which is associated with things Irish,
            would be better accepted by the audience. While
            they need not be exactly alike, all four should be
            dressed in bright green, including hats or caps of
            some kind. The pig could be either hand- or
            mouth-action, but the latter would be more effec-
            tive.

SETTING: The change of scene from the leprechaun's domain
            to the site of the dance is accomplished by the
            leprechaun and pig exiting in one direction and
            reentering from the other. No prop stage is
            needed.

PROPS: The shoe is the only prop. A doll's shoe could be
            used, or a small slipper could be made of felt.

TAPING: The sound effect of the hammer tapping and
            being thrown could be made by a real hammer.
            The leprechaun's voice should be that of a grouchy
            old man, and the pig's should be low and pleasant.
            Plenty of time should be allowed for the two
            puppets to exit and reenter when the scene
            changes. Some kind of pipe music, perhaps flute
            or even ocarina, could be used at the beginning of
            the play and reprised at the end for the lepre-
            chauns' dance. If a tape or record is used, it should
            be something lilting and recognizable as Irish

dance music. It should not go on so long that the audience will become bored.

ACTION: The puppeteer on the right should be the leprechaun. This puppet should enter right and toss the shoe backstage to the left where it can be retrieved when needed. The puppeteer on the left can operate the tape player and be the pig. The pig enters left and exits the same way to arrange the dance. After picking up the shoe (from the puppeteer's free hand), the leprechaun exits right to resume work until summoned by the pig who has reentered left. Then both puppets exit left and, after a brief pause, reenter from the right. The pig's final exit is to the left. The puppeteer must remove the pig and wear leprechaun puppets on both hands. The other puppeteer must use the fourth leprechaun puppet. The three leprechauns enter, one by one, to join the first, who is already dancing. The bodies should be held erect and the arms down (as well as possible). The movement should be up and down with some slight shifts left and right. Finally, as the music fades, they should turn to exit right in single file, still dancing. The dance should be practiced until the puppets perform in unison.

TIME: 7 $^1/_2$ minutes. Allow extra time for introductory music and for the dance at the end.

THE TRICKY EASTER BUNNY

CHARACTERS

NARRATOR
EASTER BUNNY
GIRL
BOY
SCAMP, A DOG

PROPS

2 EASTER BASKETS
2 BAGS OF JELLYBEANS

NARRATOR: One sunny spring afternoon a rabbit hopped into the garden behind a little white house. . . . (*Easter Bunny enters*) . . . This rabbit was very much larger than the brown cottontails you usually see in your yard, because he was, in fact, the Easter Bunny. First he hopped to the farthest corner of the garden where the daffodils were in full flower . . . and then he hopped to the opposite corner where the tulips were just starting to bloom. . . . All the while he glanced this way and that, as if he were searching for something.

EASTER BUNNY: Easter's coming! Easter's coming tomorrow, so this is my last chance to take a good look around this bee-yoo-tiful garden. Last year those two kids who live here found their Easter baskets much too easily. This year I don't want that to happen. . . . Uh-oh! Someone's coming. I'd better hide behind this juniper bush. (*hides to one side. . . . girl and boy enter*)

GIRL: Tomorrow will be Easter. I sure hope the Easter Bunny won't forget to come.

BOY: He never forgets, and he always hides our baskets in this part of the garden.

GIRL: Yes, I always find mine in the center of the rose bed, hardly hidden at all.

BOY: And I always find mine under the forsythia bush.

GIRL: Silly old bunny. He hides them in the same place every year.

BOY: We'll know eactly where to look tomorrow morning. Come on, let's go get our baskets. (*girl and boy exit*)

EASTER BUNNY: Hah! Call me a silly old bunny, will you? Just you wait and see who's silly.

NARRATOR: The Easter Bunny was very angry indeed. He poked around the garden a bit more until suddenly he had an inspiration. Then, since his busiest time of year was coming up, he hopped away chuckling to himself. (*Easter Bunny exits*) . . . Later, right before they went to bed, the kids left their baskets outside on the back step for the Easter Bunny to find. (*girl and boy enter, put down baskets, and exit*)

* * * * * * * *

NARRATOR: Early the net morning the Easter Bunny returned carrying fancy eggs and other Easter treats. (*Easter Bunny enters with jellybean-filled bags that he sets down*)

EASTER BUNNY: It's been a long, hard night, and I'm worn to a frazzle. Now those kids are about to learn that I'm a tricky bunny, not a silly bunny. . . . Well, I see their baskets are here waiting to be filled. Allrighty, here's something for you . . . (*puts a bag into one basket*) . . . and something for you, too. . . . (*puts a bag into other basket*) . . . And now, heh-heh-heh, I'll put my tricky plan into effect.

NARRATOR: Then that tricky bunny began to dig a hole between two lilac bushes. . . . (*bunny digs frantically*) . . . As everyone knows, rabbits are excellent diggers, so this took him only a minute. Then, into that hole went the first basket. (*bunny plants basket*) . . . and the second basket soon followed. (*bunny plants second basket*) . . . Now there was nothing left to do but to cover the baskets with leaves and twigs. Then, his dastardly deed done, the Easter Bunny hid behind the juniper bush. (*bunny hides to one side*) . . . It was none too soon, because the girl and boy were up early, and of course the first thing they wanted to do was to search for their Easter baskets. (*girl and boy enter*)

GIRL: I know where to look for my basket. Right smack in the middle of the rose garden.

BOY: And mine will be under the forsythia, as usual. (*they begin to search*)

GIRL: Oh, mine isn't where I thought it would be.

BOY: Mine either. I can't find it anywhere.

GIRL: (*crying*) The Easter Bunny forgot us.

BOY: It's worse than that. Where are our baskets? I'll bet he took them away to give to someone else.

GIRL: The Easter Bunny doesn't like us any more. (*sobs*)

BOY: Here comes Scamp. . . . (*dog enters and licks kids' faces*) . . . Good old dog! You still love us, even if the Easter Bunny doesn't. (*dog begins to snoop and sniff around the garden*)

GIRL: Whatever is Scamp doing? He's sniffing around those two lilac bushes . . . (*dog digs*) . . . and now he's digging like crazy. Naughty Scamp! You know you're not supposed to dig in the garden.

BOY: Maybe he buried a bone there. Is that what you did, Scamp?

SCAMP: Woof! Woof! (*exits*)

GIRL: Well, there goes Scamp. I guess it wasn't a bone after all. But something must be in that hole, and

	I'm going to see what it is. . . . (*looks into hole*) . . . Why, it's our Easter baskets! . . . Here's mine, good as new. (*retrieves basket*) . . .
BOY:	Oh, let me see. Let me see. . . . (*looks into hole*) . . . Yes, sure enough, mine's here too. Out of my way! Let me at it. (*retrieves basket*) . . .
GIRL:	This is all very strange. I wonder how our Easter baskets ended up in a hole.
BOY:	I guess we'll never know the answer to that. Well, let's take them inside where they'll be safe. (*girl and boy exit with baskets*)
NARRATOR:	Leaving the garden that girl and boy were all smiles, and you can be sure that Scamp got an Easter treat, too. . . . (*Easter Bunny moves center stage*) . . . After working all night that poor old rabbit was exhausted, and he planned to go home and sleep for a week.
EASTER BUNNY:	(*addresses audience*) But confidentially, just between you all and me, I'm really pleased that those kids found their Easter baskets after all. And I can be pretty sure that they'll never call me a "silly old bunny" again. From now on I'm the "Tricky Easter Bunny!" (*hops away*)

The Tricky Easter Bunny

Production notes

PUPPETS: The girl and boy must be hand-action puppets as the script requires them to carry their Easter baskets. The Easter Bunny and dog may be either hand- or mouth-action puppets, because their digging can be suggested by shaking their bodies, and the Easter Bunny can manipulate props using either mouth or paws.

SETTING: No actual flowers or bushes are needed to suggest the garden setting, but a prop stage, either permanent or temporary, is necessary so that the girl and boy can set down their baskets and the Easter Bunny his two bags of jellybeans. The "hole" is out of audience vision, behind the puppet stage and is, of course, the waiting hand of a puppeteer.

PROPS: If small baskets are unavailable, they could be fashioned from sturdy brown corrugated cardboard. They should have rigid, highly arched handles which are easy for the puppets to manipulate, allowing for quick insertion of the jellybeans. The bags holding the few jellybeans should be of clear plastic, securely tied at the top with enough surplus so that the Easter Bunny can carry them.

TAPING: No special sound effects are needed. The girl puppet's voice should be high, the boy's medium, and the rabbit's low. The narrator may be any good reader. If music is used at the beginning, it may be reprised to show the passage of time between Easter Eve when the children put their baskets outside and the following morning when the Bunny returns.

ACTION: The action is easy to manage, because much of it is described by the narrator or the characters themselves as it happens. Note that when the children converse, the girl always speaks first. The puppeteer on the left should work the tape player and take the parts of both girl and boy who will enter and exit from that side (their house). The puppeteer on the right should be the Easter Bunny and Scamp. The Bunny should enter and exit from the right and Scamp from the left since he lives with the children. After the dog's brief appearance, there is just enough time allowed so that the puppeteer can remove the puppet and be handed the Easter baskets when they are put into the hole one at a time. Later they can be handed to the children in the same way.

TIME: 6 $^1/_2$ minutes, which includes 15 seconds for nighttime interim during which some music could be used. Allow extra time for introductory music.

GRACIE'S GARDEN

CHARACTERS

DADDY
GRACIE

PROPS

SHOVEL
SPOON
PACKET OF SEEDS
BOX OF MAGIC-GROW
GIANT FLOWER

(*Father enters with shovel and begins to dig*)

GRACIE: (*enters*) Daddy! Daddy! What are you doing?

DADDY: I'm doing a special springtime job, Gracie. I'm digging a vegetable garden.

GRACIE: Oh, goody! Can I help?

DADDY: No, but you may watch.

GRACIE: But, Daddy, I want to help.

DADDY: This shovel is too big for you, but I have an idea.

GRACIE: What's that?

DADDY: You can plant your own garden. Do you think you'd like that?

GRACIE: Oh, yes!

DADDY: All right then, go into the house and get a big spoon to dig with.

GRACIE: I'll do that. Don't go away. I'll be right back. (*exits*)

DADDY: And I will be right here digging. (*digs*)

GRACIE: (*enters with spoon*) I'm back. Where should I dig my garden, Daddy?

41

DADDY: (*looks*) Well, let me think a minute. . . . Oh, I know. While I'm digging a big garden for vegetables here by the garage, you can dig a little garden for flowers near the back door. How's that?

GRACIE: Fine. Flowers are much, much nicer than vegetables.

DADDY: Let's get to work then. (*they begin to dig*)

GRACIE: I think a little working song would help me get done faster. (*sings while digging*) This is the way I dig my garden, dig my garden, dig my garden. This is the way I dig my garden, so early in the morning. . . . (*stops digging*) That working song really did help. I'm all done digging.

DADDY: My goodness, you *are* fast.

GRACIE: What comes next?

DADDY: Net comes planting your seeds.

GRACIE: But I don't have any seeds.

DADDY: There are packets of seeds inside the house on the kitchen table. There are seeds for growing cucumbers and squash and carrots and radishes and lettuce, and there is also a packet of flower seeds. You may have that one for your garden. Why don't you go in and get it now? Just be sure to pick the one that says "Flower Seeds" on the envelope.

GRACIE: Now, Daddy, you know I can't read.

DADDY: You can read the picture on the front of the packet, even if you can't read the print. Just remember that if the picture on the front looks like a cucumber, cucumbers are what will come up from the seeds.

GRACIE: Well, I certainly don't want any cucumbers in my garden. I'll be sure that there's a picture of flowers

	on what I plant. Don't go away. I'll be right back. (*exits with spoon*)
DADDY:	And I'll still be right here digging. (*digs*)
GRACIE:	(*enters with packet*) Here I am back again. I found the right packet of seeds. See all the pretty flowers?
DADDY:	Yes, that's the right one. You can sow the seeds now. Sprinkle them evenly and carefully.
GRACIE:	I will. . . . I'm sure another little working song will help. (*sings while planting*) This is the way I sow my seeds, sow my seeds, sow my seeds. This is the way I sow my seeds, so early in the morning. . . . There, I'm done. All of my seeds are planted. . . . I'd better throw this envelope away inside. I don't want any litter in my garden. (*exits with empty packet . . . enters*) . . . Daddy, are you almost finished with your digging?
DADDY:	Yes. I'm going to put my shovel away now and get my fertilizer. (*exits with shovel . . . returns with box of Magic-Grow*) This Magic-Grow should make my garden shoot up like crazy. (*shakes Magic-Grow over garden*) . . .
GRACIE:	Oh, let me have some, too.
DADDY:	Magic-Grow should really go in before you plant seeds, not after. I think your flowers will grow just fine without it.
GRACIE:	Daddy, please give me some Magic-Grow. I want my garden to shoot up like crazy, too.
DADDY:	Oh, all right, Gracie. There's some left in the box. It's just the right amount for your garden, so here you are. It's all yours. (*hands box to Gracie*) When the box is empty, pat the ground gently to cover your seeds.
GRACIE:	I will, I will, I will.

DADDY: Be sure to sprinkle it evenly and carefully. Magic-Grow is powerful stuff.

GRACIE: All right. I'll be careful.

DADDY: That's my good girl. Well, Gracie, there are other things I must do today, so I have to leave you now. I'll be back later. (*exits*)

GRACIE: Good-bye, Daddy. . . . And now to sprinkle the Magic-Grow on my garden, evenly and carefully the way Daddy told me to. . . . My, this big box is hard to handle. (*struggles with box, which upends*) Oops! (*wails*) Oh, dear! It spilled out of the box, and all in one spot. I didn't mean to do that. Now my garden will be ruined. (*sobs*) I wish I'd never heard of Magic-Grow. I'm going to get rid of this nasty box right now. (*exits with box . . . enters*) Well, even if my garden is ruined, I guess I'd better pat the ground gently to cover the seeds . . . Maybe, just maybe, something might grow after all. A little working song might not help, but it couldn't hurt. (*sings sadly while patting*) This is the way I pat the ground, pat the ground, pat the ground. This is the way I pat the ground, so early in the morning. . . (*stops patting*) There, I'm done. Now all I can do is hope for the best . . . Hey, what's that? . . . (*strange noise begins*) I hear a funny noise. . . . It seems to be coming from my garden. . . . Yes, it is. It's coming from the spot where I spilled the Magic-Grow. . . . It's getting louder!
. . . And now I see something poking out of the ground at that spot. . . . Oh, what is that thing? . . . Oooooooh. (*watches as giant flower grows toward top of stage*) . . . It's a monster flower! Daddy was right. Magic-Grow is powerful stuff. (*looks up at flower . . . Gracie and flower sway in unison . . . this way . . . and that . . . this way . . . and that*) I'm getting dizzy. (*stands quietly*) . . . That's better. . . . Oh, I have an idea. I think this giant flower

would make a fine springtime surprise for my mother. I'll just pick it and take it in to her. (*struggles with flower*) Easy to say, but not so easy to do. (*struggles and finally picks flower*) There! I did it! (*shouts*) Mommy! Mommy! I have a surprise for you. . . . I hope you have a *really* big vase. (*exits*)

Gracie's Garden

PUPPETS: Both characters should be flexible hand-action puppets in order to manipulate the props. For credibility's sake Gracie, who is supposed to be very young, should be noticeably smaller than the father puppet.

SETTING: No prop stage is needed to indicate that all of the action takes place in the backyard between the house and garage.

PROPS: While a toy shovel would be best, a small pancake turner would work for Daddy's shovel. Gracie's spoon can be either a teaspoon or a tablespoon. The seed envelope should have flowers on the front and a corner already torn off. An open Jell-O™ box (large size) can be covered with paper and designated "Magic-Grow" in large letters. The flower must have a stem taller than Gracie. It could be a thin dowel painted green with a few paper leaves and a flower on top.

TAPING: Daddy's voice should be slow and patient, Gracie's piping. Gracie's unaccompanied working songs are to the tune of "The Mulberry Bush." Pauses during brief exits must be long enough to allow time for the necessary action. Plenty of time should also be allowed for Gracie and the flower to sway in unison. The noise the flower makes should begin softly and increase in volume. It could be a slurping or gurgling noise or even scratching.

ACTION: The puppeteer on the left should be Gracie. All of her entrances and exits should be made at the left (the house) except for the one in which she disposes of the Magic-Grow box, which should be done at stage right. Daddy's entrances and exits are all at the right (the garage). The puppeteer at the left who manipulates Gracie should hold the flower in the other hand in order to synchronize the swaying motions. Either puppeteer can operate the tape player.

TIME: 8 minutes. Allow extra time for introductory music.

THE PICNIC

CHARACTERS

NARRATOR
GIRL
RABBIT
SQUIRREL
RACCOON
BOY

PROPS

BUTTERFLY
BASKET
CARROT STICKS
PEACH
PLASTIC WRAP
PAPER BAG

NARRATOR: Summertime. . . . A time for going to the beach, splashing in the waves, and building sand castles. . . . A time for going to the park, playing ball, and chasing butterflies. . . . A time for roller skates and bikes and swings. . . . And most of all, a time for picnics. . . . Here comes a picnicker now.

GIRL: (*enters with basket*) What a day! This has to be the best day of the whole year. Gorgeous, simply gor-*geous*! On such a perfect summer day, I had to plan a picnic . . . even if . . . even if . . . even if I have to go picnicking all by myself. (*whimpers*) But, no, I'm not going to be unhappy today. If all of my friends are away on vacation, it's their tough luck. I will have a lovely picnic anyway. (*looks about*) This seems like a good spot. I'll put my basket under this giant oak tree. (*sets down basket*) Yes, this will be just right. And I'll put myself down next to the basket. (*settles near basket . . . sound of bird chirping . . . looks up*) Hello, birdie. Have you come to join me on my picnic? (*chirps fade away*) I guess not, so, good-bye, birdie. (*butterfly appears*) Hello, butterfly. (*watches butter-*

48

fly flutter away) Good-bye, butterfly. (*sighs*) Even the birds and butterflies are heading off on vacations. . . . It's no use. I'm not in the mood for a picnic. Maybe in a little while I'll feel like eating the good lunch I brought. But first, I think I'll take a walk to work up an appetite. Perhaps I'll even wade in the little brook at the edge of the woods. That seems like a good thing to do on a summer day. (*exits . . . bird chirps . . . butterfly flutters across stage*)

NARRATOR: Our heroine is off to cool her feet in the brook, leaving the picnic basket behind. I wonder if that was a good idea. . . . (*rabbit enters*) Here comes a rabbit, and he has his eye on the basket. Perhaps there is something inside that would appeal to a rabbit. Well, we're about to find out. He's looking things over very carefully. . . . Aha! I think he's found something. Yes, there are carrot sticks in the basket, and everyone knows that bunnies love carrots. Maybe that's why carrots are called rabbit food. . . . My goodness, this fellow is really hungry. Munch, crunch, those carrot sticks are going . . . going . . . gone, and the rabbit is leaving, too. (*rabbit exits . . . bird chirps . . . butterfly flutters across stage*) Do I hear a noise up above? Yes, it's the squirrel who lives in the old oak tree. (*squirrel enters*) She must have an eye on that picnic basket, too, and she's wondering if there's anything inside that a squirrel might like. . . . I think she's found something. Could there be nuts in that picnic lunch? . . . No, it's a peach. Squirrels are very fond of fruit. . . . Mmmmm, that peach must taste good. I didn't think a squirrel could eat so fast. . . . Well, she's finished her treat, so off she goes, up the tree in a flash. (*squirrel exits . . . bird chirps . . . butterfly flutters across stage*) Oh, no, here comes another uninvited guest. (*raccoon enters*) Of course, he's headed right for the picnic basket. . . . Hey, Mr. Raccoon, do you see anything you'd like? . . . That was a silly question. Raccoons are always hungry, and they are not fussy eaters. This guy seems to be eating everything that's left in the basket. . . . Potato chips. . . . Sandwiches. . . . Cookies. . . . What terrible table manners! (*shouts*) Hey, shame on you for making such a mess. . . . Well, I believe he's finished. There he goes. (*raccoon exits . . . bird chirps . . . butterfly flutters by*) Uh-oh, look who's returning to eat her lunch.

GIRL: (*enters*) Wading in that pretty little brook gave me an appetite. Now I'll really enjoy my picnic. (*looks into basket*) Oh, no! The food is all gone. There's nothing left but crumbs and a peach seed and the plastic from around my sandwiches. Who would be mean enough to steal a kid's picnic lunch? (*whimpers*) My day is ruined. (*cries*) . . . But I know that crying won't help, so I might as well try to cheer up. I'll go back home to eat. (*starts to pick up basket*)

BOY: (*enters with paper bag*) Hi, there.

GIRL: Hello.

BOY: Are you another picnicker?

GIRL: I planned to have a picnic, but somebody stole my lunch when my back was turned.

BOY: Gee, that's too bad.

GIRL: My day is ruined, so I'm going home.

BOY: Please don't leave. I have plenty of food for two.

GIRL: Well, I don't know. . . .

BOY: Oh, come on and share my lunch. I have sandwiches, carrot sticks, potato chips, and cookies and fruit for desert.

GIRL: Why, that's exactly what I had in my basket. . . .

	Say, you aren't the one who stole my picnic lunch, are you?
BOY:	Oh, no. I wouldn't do anything like that. But there are lots of animals around here who might eat a picnic lunch, and I just saw a raccoon licking peanut butter off his whiskers.
GIRL:	I'll bet you're right about animals eating my lunch. I *did* bring peanut butter and jelly sandwiches.
BOY:	Well, mine are tuna fish.
GIRL:	Mmmmm, tuna is my favorite.
BOY:	How about it then? I packed plenty of food in case I met one of my friends along the way. But all of my friends are away on vacation.
GIRL:	Mine are, too. I guess that means you're my new friend. So, thank you very much, I'll be happy to share your lunch. There's a nice little brook I want to show you first though. It's perfect for wading.
BOY:	I think we'll take the lunch with us.
GIRL:	Yes, the animals have already had their picnic. (*they exit, the girl taking the basket with her*)
NARRATOR:	So two new friends are off to enjoy the perfect summer day, and one thing is sure . . . they're not going to—let that lunch out of their sight. (*bird chirps . . . butterfly flutters across stage*)

The Picnic

Production notes

PUPPETS: All of the puppets, even the animals, should be hand-action. The more of the animals' bodies that shows, the better. Unless someone is very adept at puppet making, the animal puppets, especially the squirrel, might best be purchased from a professional supplier.

SETTING: The setting remains the same throughout. A prop stage is necessary to hold the picnic basket for the play's duration. If this is a temporary one, it should be placed near the side frame of the puppet stage, which represents the oak tree.

PROPS: The butterfly should be made of brightly colored paper and attached to a black thread, which will not show against the black backdrop. If a small basket with a handle is not available, one could be made from brown cardboard. Since it must remain in place throughout the play, it would be a good idea to put a piece of sticky tape on the bottom to keep it in place. The carrot sticks can be made from rolled orange paper, and the peach from Play-Doh™. Any kind of plastic wrap could be wadded up and used for the discarded sandwich wrappings. The paper bag, a small one, should be filled with wadded paper and tied at the top.

TAPING: The only sound effect is the bird's chirping, which may be done by anyone who can whistle. This should be very brief, and several seconds of silence should be allowed for the butterfly's appearances. The girl's voice should be higher in pitch than the boy's, and the narrator can be any good reader.

ACTION:

The puppeteer on the right should be the girl and all of the animals. After the girl's first entrance from the left, she should cross stage and put down the basket. Her remaining exits and entrances are at the right. After the girl's first exit, the puppeteer should remove the puppet and use the other (right) hand for all of the animal puppets in turn. The animals should enter from the right, the squirrel sliding down the puppet stage frame (or curtain) from above, as if from the tree. The animals can lift the (food and paper) props from the basket in order for the audience to see them, and then replace them while seeming to eat. The animals all exit right. The puppeteer on the left should operate the tape player, manage the butterfly (from above), and take the part of the boy, who should enter from the left and exit right.

TIME:

7 minutes. Allow extra time for introductory music.

AUTUMN LEAVES

CHARACTERS

CHILD/NARRATOR
SQUIRREL
RACCOON
FOX
SKUNK

PROPS

AUTUMN LEAVES
PINE CONE
RAKE

CHILD: *(enters . . . puppets appear as described in monologue)*
Autumn leaves are falling down.
Some are gold, and some are brown.
Others are of flaming red
Floating gently 'round my head. . . .
    Oh, so gently 'round my head. . . .
I think I'll wander off today
Along the path that leads this way
Into the woods where I may meet
Some furry friends, if I'm discreet.
    I'll try my best to be discreet. . . .
Hi, there, Ms. Squirrel, from what I hear
The pinecone crop is good this year.
You're busy gathering them, I see,
So please continue. Don't mind me.
    Yes, hurry on and don't mind me. . . .
Who's this behind a bandit's mask?
It's Sir Raccoon—I needn't ask.
That's no disguise, for I can tell
It's you. And, Sir, it suits you well.
    Indeed, it suits you very well. . . .
And now who's coming down the trail?
It's Fox, another bushy tail.
Let's visit. What? No time to spend?

Oh, very well, be off, my friend,
    Until another day, my friend. . . .
Oops! Mrs. Skunk, I hope you're fine.
Forgive me if I'm out of line,
But knowing what you sometimes do,
I think I'll back away from you.
    In fact, I'll *run* away from you! . . .
Yes, autumn leaves are falling down,
Gold and red, but mostly brown.
Too bad! That means that I must take
The path back home. It's time to rake.
    It's time to rake and rake and rake. . . .
(exits and returns with rake)

Autumn Leaves

Production notes

PUPPETS: The child, which may be either a girl or a boy, should be a hand-action puppet. The animals could be either hand- or mouth-action, but they should have bodies that will be visible to the audience.

SETTING: The passing animals suggest the woodsy setting.

PROPS: The leaves may be torn bits of construction paper or tissue paper in appropriate colors. The pinecone (real) should be a size that the squirrel can easily carry in its mouth or paws. The rake can be made of a thin dowel with fanned strips of cardboard for rake teeth.

TAPING: The child has the only speaking part. The person who records this role should speak slowly and distinctly, paying careful attention to the punctuation. It will be important to the action to allow several seconds between the verses so that the animals can enter and exit.

ACTION: The puppeteer on the left should take the part of the child and also sprinkle the leaves from above. The child should enter from the left and not progress beyond center stage. This puppet can move back slightly to let each animal pass by and should exit left to get the rake with which he or she reenters to take his or her bow. The puppeteer on the right should start the tape player and act as all the animals. Animal exits must be made on the fourth line of each stanza so that the net role may be assumed. With one exception the animals should all enter from the right, pause briefly to acknowledge the child, and continue on to exit left. The exception is the skunk who can turn and exit right so that the child can seem to run away by moving left.

TIME: 2 1/2 minutes. Allow extra time for introductory music.

HALLOWEEN GHOSTS

CHARACTERS

ANNABELLE
TIMOTHY
SMALL CHILD
GHOST

PROPS

SHEET
3 GHOST COSTUMES
3 TREAT BAGS

(*Annabelle and Timothy enter from opposite sides, bumping into each other at center stage*)

ANNABELLE: Ouch! (*clutches head*) Oh, that hurts. . . . Why, it's Timothy Jones! Well, Timothy, why don't you watch where you're going?

TIMOTHY: Oh, hi, Annabelle. I'm sorry, but I was thinking about something else, and I just didn't notice you walking down the street. Come to think of it, why don't *you* watch where *you're* going?

ANNABELLE: To tell the truth, I was thinking about something, too, and I didn't notice you either.

TIMOTHY: Are you really hurt?

ANNABELLE: No, I'm all right. What were you thinking about that's so important?

TIMOTHY: Halloween.

ANNABELLE: No kidding? That's what I was thinking about, too. Halloween is almost here.

TIMOTHY:
That's the trouble. It's coming up all too soon. Trick-or-treating is one of my favorite things to do, and I don't have a costume.

ANNABELLE:
Me either. I've been thinking about it all week, but I still haven't decided what I'm going to wear.

TIMOTHY:
So far all I know is that I'm going to make my costume myself.

ANNABELLE:
I think I will, too. Homemade costumes are much better than the kind you buy at a store.

TIMOTHY:
(*laughing*) Especially if you've already spent your allowance on something else.

ANNABELLE:
Hey, I just had a thought. My mom has some old white sheets at home. Maybe I'll be a ghost.

TIMOTHY:
That's not very original. Lots of people dress up like ghosts.

ANNABELLE:
But what could be more like Halloween than a ghost? And a ghost costume would be easy to make. After all, there's not enough time to make anything fancier.

TIMOTHY:
You're right about that. Well, *your* problem is solved. I'm right back where I started. I still don't know what I'll be on Halloween.

ANNABELLE:
Timothy, my mom really has *lots* of old white sheets. If you want to be a ghost, too, I'll give you a sheet to make a costume.

TIMOTHY:
You will? Wonderful!

ANNABELLE:
If you want to, you can come home with me now, and I'll give you the sheet right away.

TIMOTHY: Thanks, Annabelle. I guess *my* problem is taken care of, too. Let's go. (*They exit . . . and Timothy reenters carrying sheet*) This sheet is all I need to turn myself into a scary Halloween ghost. I'll go home and work on the costume now. It shouldn't take long, and while I'm doing that, I can practice making spooky ghost noises. (*exits*) . . . oooo-OOOOOOOooo . . . ooooOOOOOooooo . . . ooooooooOOOOOOOOooooooooo . . .

* * * * * * * *

ANNABELLE: (*enters wearing ghost costume and carrying treat bag*) I'm ready to go trick-or-treating. Maybe I'm early. I haven't seen any other kids yet.

TIMOTHY: (*enters wearing ghost costume and carrying treat bag*) oooooOOOOOOOooooooooo.

ANNABELLE: (*backing away*) Timothy, is that you?

TIMOTHY: (*laughing*) Yes. I scared you, didn't I? I've been practicing making spooky ghost noises. ooooOOOOOOooooo . . . You try it, too. Then we can go and ring some doorbells.

ANNABELLE: All right. How does this sound? oooooooooo-oooo . . .

TIMOTHY: Not so good. You have to start soft and low. Then, little by little, go higher and louder. And then finally let it fade away in the night . . . like this . . . oooooooOOOOOOOoooooo . . . ooooooOOOOOOOOooooo . . . Why don't you try it again?

ANNABELLE: Okay . . . oooooOOOOOOOOOooooo . . . How's that?

TIMOTHY: That's better. Try it once more.

ANNABELLE: oooooOOOOOOoooOOOOOOOOOOooooooooo.

TIMOTHY: *Very* good! I couldn't do better myself. Now I'm going to start ringing doorbells. Are you coming with me?

ANNABELLE: Yes, that would be much more fun than going alone.

TIMOTHY: And so the fun begins!

ANNABELLE: Yes, ringing bells and scaring people.

TIMOTHY: And even better, getting lots and lots of Halloween treats.

ANNABELLE: Timothy, I see someone coming.

TIMOTHY: Ah, yes. It's a pint-sized trick-or-treater. Now to test my spooky ghost noises. . . . (*small child enters wearing costume and carrying treat bag*) oooOOOOO-oooooo . . . oooooooOOOOOOOOooooooooo . . .

SMALL CHILD: Help! Help! (*turns and exits*)

TIMOTHY: (*laughing*) How about that, Annabelle? What a riot! That kid thought we were real ghosts. Did you see him run?

ANNABELLE: Yes, Timothy, but that was mean. The poor kid was really scared. I think I should go after him. (*starts to follow the child*) . . . Hey, little boy, where are you?

SMALL CHILD: (*enters and races across stage*) Help! Help! (*exits*)

ANNABELLE: (*calls after him*) Come back, little boy. We're not ghosts. We're just trick-or-treaters like you. We won't hurt you, honest.

SMALL CHILD:	(*enters and recrosses stage*) Help! Help! Mommy, Mommy, Mommy! Some bad ghosts are after me. (*exits . . . door slams*)
ANNABELLE:	Little boy, little boy, please come back. Oh, dear.
TIMOTHY:	Give it up, Annabelle. Didn't you hear his front door slam? He's safe at home now where we bad ghosts can't get him. But meanwhile our treat bags are empty. So let's get started.
ANNABELLE:	Yes, let's! We can go up one side of the street and down the other and hit every house.
TIMOTHY:	I think it would be better to crisscross the street, and that way we can go right around the block.
ANNABELLE:	That's fine with me. ooooooOOOOOOOO-ooooooo . . .
TIMOTHY:	Let's start here. (*moves side stage followed by Annabelle. . . .doorbell chimes . . . presents treat bag*) Trick or treat. . . Thank you very much.
ANNABELLE:	(*presents treat bag*) Trick or treat. . . . Thank you.
TIMOTHY:	Now to cross the street. . . . oooooOOOOOO-ooooo . . . (*crosses stage followed by Annabelle. . . . doorbell chimes. . . . presents treat bag*) Trick or treat. . . . Thank you.
ANNABELLE:	(*presents treat bag*) Trick or treat. . . . Thank you.
TIMOTHY:	Let's cross the street again. . . . ooooOOOOOoooo . . . (*crosses stage followed by Annabelle. . . . doorbell chimes. . . . presents treat bag*) Trick or treat. . . . Thank you.
ANNABELLE:	(*presents treat bag*) Trick or treat. . . . Thank you very much.

TIMOTHY: See, this is working out just right. Let's cross over. . . . oooooOOOOOOooooo . . . (*crosses stage followed by Annabelle. . . . doorbell chimes. . . . presents treat bag*) Trick or treat . . . Thanks a lot.

ANNABELLE: (*presents treat bag*) Trick or treat. . . . Thank you very much.

TIMOTHY: Only one more house till we turn the corner. Time to cross the street again. . . . oooooOOOOOOOO-oooooo . . . (*crosses stage followed by Annabelle. . . . doorbell chimes. . . . presents treat bag*) Trick or treat. . . . Thank you.

ANNABELLE: (*presents treat bag*) Trick or treat. . . . Thank you.

TIMOTHY: This is going just the way I expected, Annabelle. Crisscrossing the street was a good idea.

ANNABELLE: (*looking into bag*) And we're getting good treats, too. We've been to five houses, and I have five different kinds of candy bars.

TIMOTHY: And they're all chocolate. Yum-yum. Chocolate is my favorite.

ANNABELLE: I like it best, too. . . . Say, Timothy, look down the street. I see another trick-or-treater headed this way.

TIMOTHY: (*looks*) You're right. It's someone else dressed as a ghost, too. Here he comes now.

GHOST: (*enters*) oooooOOOOOOOOOooooo.

TIMOTHY: Hi, fellow ghost. How is your trick-or-treating going?

GHOST: oooooooOOOOOOOOOOoooooooo.

TIMOTHY: Don't go ooooOOOOOOOooooooo to me. I know
                how to make spooky ghost noises, too, and so does
                Annabelle. So, how are you doing?

GHOST: oooooooOOOOOOOOOOOOOooooooooooo.

ANNABELLE: Timothy, look! This ghost doesn't have a treat
                bag.

GHOST: oooooOOOOOOOOoooooooooo.

TIMOTHY: You're right! Th-th-th-that could only mean one
                thing. This is a real ghost. I'm out of here. (*exits*)

ANNABELLE: Wait for me. (*exits*)

GHOST: oooooOOOOOOOoooooooo . . . (*shakes off sheet
                revealing small child in costume, still carrying treat
                bag*)

SMALL CHILD: Mommy was right. Those bad ghosts weren't real
                ghosts after all. Now it's *my* turn to get some
                treats. (*moves side-stage. . . . doorbell chimes. . . .
                presents treat bag*) Trick or treat. . . . Thank you.

Halloween Ghosts

Production notes

PUPPETS:
Only three hand-action puppets are needed, since the ghost character is actually the small child in disguise. Timothy and Annabelle should be compatible in size and appearance, and the small child should be noticeably smaller. He should be wearing a black half-mask and carrying a treat bag to indicate that he is dressed for Halloween at his first entrance.

SETTING:
Nothing special is needed to indicate the street scene setting, and since the puppets always keep their props in hand, a prop stage is unnecessary.

PROPS:
A square foot of white cloth will suffice for the sheet that Timothy carries across the stage. The ghost costumes of the two main characters should consist of two round-at-the-top pieces of white material sewn together with big slits for the arms. They should fit loosely. Elongated black ovals can be drawn (or glued on) for eyes and mouths. The small child's ghost costume should be a circle of white cloth about 30 inches in diameter, which will allow the puppet to rise high enough to seem a real ghost. There should be a suggestion of eyes and mouth on this, too. The treat bags can be made of orange cloth or paper, but the handles should be heavy cord that can be attached to the puppets' hands with tape or pins.

TAPING:
Besides the ghost noises made by the characters, there are several sound effects. The door slam need

be nothing more than a hand hitting a tabletop. Unless real chimes are available, a toy piano, xylophone, or even a buzzer could be used for the doorbell sounds. The voice that records Timothy's role should be much lower than the one that records Annabelle's, and the small child's should be the highest pitch. The ghost sounds should be drawn out, increasing in volume, and then fading away, as is described in one speech. The stage directions should be kept in mind during taping, with the indicated pauses carefully observed to allow adequate time for the action. Halloween music used at the beginning may be reprised to show the passage of time between the day of the first action and Halloween night.

ACTION: The puppeteer on the left should start the tape player and take the role of Timothy, leaving the puppeteer on the right to take the other two roles. It is easier to remember the sides of subsequent entrances and exits by recalling that the characters' homes are supposed to be in the direction of their initial entrances. So Timothy first enters from the left and Annabelle from the right. They exit right to get the sheet, which Timothy carries across the stage to exit left. Intermission music will allow time for the ghost costumes to be donned. Later the puppeteer at left can help to drape the child's ghost costume across this puppet during the repeated stage crossings. The small child enters, turns, and makes his first exit at right, then crosses the stage exiting and reentering left, and finally crosses and exits right (his house). His last entrance is from the right, and once the other characters run away, the puppeteer merely shakes the ghost costume off his hand, letting it fall backstage. For their Halloween visits, Timothy and Annabelle simply crisscross the stage, beginning at the right. They should thrust the bags behind the side curtain for their imaginary treats.

TIME: 13 minutes. This does not include time for introductory music to be played or for the brief intermission during which the music may be reprised.

WITCHES AND GHOSTS

CHARACTERS   **PROP**

    WITCH   LIST
    GHOST

(*Witch and Ghost enter from opposite sides, bow to each other, and face audience, swaying from side to side as they begin*)

BOTH: On the night of Halloween
Lots of witches and ghosts are seen.

WITCH: I'm a witch,

GHOST: and I'm a ghost.

BOTH: Who is the one that scares you most?

WITCH: Everyone knows that I'm the scariest creature that anyone could hope to meet on a creepy, dark Halloween night.

GHOST::   Oh, you are mistaken, my friend. I'm sure that most people would agree that a spooky ghost like me is much more frightening than any ordinary, run-of-the-mill witch could be.

WITCH: Ordinary? Run-of-the-mill? How dare you?

GHOST: I dare, because I scare.

WITCH: You scare? Well, if you care,
I have a list somewhere that we can share,
A list of certain qualities that scare,
So just wait there.
I'll go and get my list, and we'll compare.

(*exits*)

GHOST: (*calls after her*)

          Don't worry. I'm not going anywhere,
          So don't despair.

WITCH: (*enters with list, which she tapes up at one side of stage*)

          I said I'd be right back, so there!
          Now, tell me, are you willing to compare?

GHOST: Yes, that seems fair.
          We'll soon find out which one of us can
          really scare. . . .

WITCH: Well, to compare, let's have some fun.
          We'll check this list, and when we're done,
          We'll prove who's scariest, who's to shun.

GHOST: Good! Let's begin with number one.

WITCH: Very well. First, let's consider appearance. My
          dress is long and completely black, except for a
          few rusty stains at the edges because of its great
          age. And the matching hat with its tall, pointed
          crown adds the perfect final touch. Did you notice
          that the brim does not completely hide my crone's
          face and wild, stringy hair?

GHOST: Yes, I have to admit in a hag's contest you'd be a
          real winner. But we're talking about scary, not
          ugly. Actually, I consider myself to be a rather
          handsome ghost, but no one can see a real face
          under this white shroud. It's not knowing that
          makes me so scary. You must agree that I have an
          air of mystery about me.

WITCH: Well, so do I. I still think I'm scarier than you.

GHOST: I can see that we're not going to agree on Scary
          Quality Number One, so let's get on with the
          list.

WITCH: Well, looks aren't everything, that is true.
          A voice can be frightening, through and
          through.

GHOST: Voices and noises! That's what we'll do
As comparison number two.

WITCH: All right. As you know, my voice is naturally unpleasant, a quality I inherited from my dear mother. So it's easy for me to speak in an ominous way at all times. I like to screech occasionally like this. (*screeches*) And, of course there's my cackling laugh. Heh-heh-heh-heh-heh-heh-heh. How's that for a blood chiller?

GHOST: Not bad, but it doesn't compare with my ghastly, ghastly moans. . . oooooooooOOOOOOOooo-OOOOOOOOoooooooooooo. . . .

WITCH: Well, that *was* pretty scary, but a few rattling bones and chains would have helped.

GHOST: I guess that was a compliment, so I thank you. But I can offer you a suggestion, too. Add some yowls and hisses. I'm sure your black cat would be glad to help with that. Well, what's next on your list?

WITCH: The way we move about, you and me,
Through the atmosphere, wild and free.

GHOST: Ah, yes, the perfect way, I see,
To make comparison number three.

WITCH: Hah! I'm bound to win on this one. Picture this: A huge, golden harvest moon in the sky, and perhaps a few bats darting about. All of a sudden I fly by on my broomstick, a perfect black silhouette superimposed against the lunar orb. Ah, I shudder to think of it!

GHOST: What *I* think is that you use too many big words.

WITCH: If I had my broomstick here, I'd show you.

GHOST: Well, I don't need a broomstick to show you how *I* get around. Watch. . . . (*moans and floats about*) . . .

WITCH: All right, all right. You've made your point.

GHOST: So what's next on this list?

WITCH: Special skills that most folks deplore,
Frightening skills that I have galore.

GHOST: Oh, yeah? I betcha I have more,
So let's compare on number four.

WITCH: Very well. Let me describe my magic skills. I can cast spells whenever I so choose. There's no end to the magic tricks I can do.

GHOST: I can walk right through a closed door. It doesn't matter if it's locked either. I can do it anyway. Why, I can even walk through a solid wall if I want to.

WITCH: I bet you can't mix up a batch of witches' brew or turn a boy into a frog.

GHOST: Maybe not, but I can haunt a house. Now that's much scarier than anything you have mentioned so far.

WITCH: It is not.

GHOST: Is, too.

WITCH: No.

GHOST: Yes.

WITCH: So far we haven't settled anything, and there's only one scary item left on my list.

GHOST: What is it? Maybe we can decide once and for all which one of us is the winner.

WITCH: I saved the best till last.

GHOST: Go on. I'm waiting.

WITCH: It's kind of a group activity.

GHOST: Like a ball game?

WITCH: No, actually it's a dance.

GHOST: Tell me more.

WITCH: Well . . . at Halloween we witches strive
              To scare the wits out of all alive
              Who happen to see our frenzied jive.

GHOST: So let's compare dancing for number five.

WITCH: What? Do you mean to say that ghosts dance?

GHOST: Of course we do, and very well, too, I might add.
              But you start first. Where do you witches hold
              your dances?

WITCH: Any field out in the country will do, just so long
              as it's well away from towns and cities. We usually
              decide on a place with some woods around and a
              few dead trees where owls can perch and our black
              cats can sit and watch the fun. Surely nothing
              could be scarier than that.

GHOST: You think not? Well, we ghosts always dance in a
              graveyard. There are plenty of owls to watch, and
              bats, too. We appear promptly at midnight, and
              then . . .

WITCH: Excuse me for interrupting, but midnight is
              known as the *witching* hour, and with good reason.
              Heh-heh-heh-heh-heh, I got you there.

GHOST: What kind of dance do you do?

WITCH: Well, first we have to get in the mood. Once
              everyone is there, we have our Halloween meet-
              ing, and then we exchange recipes for magic
              charms and witches' brew. Later, when the moon
              is exactly right, we begin the dance. First we form
              a circle around a huge bonfire. The dance starts off
              very slowly, like this. . . . (*demonstrates dance*) . . .
              We go faster, and faster, and faster, kicking up our
              heels and leaping into the air until at last we fall
              to the ground exhausted. (*falls and rises again*) . . .

	Then in the morning we climb on our broomsticks and ride home.
GHOST:	Our graveyard dance is much the same, except that it's scarier, of course. At the stroke of twelve all of the assembled ghosts begin to dance, slowly at first, like this. . . . (*demonstrates dance*) . . . The wind begins to blow, and we moan. . . . oooooooOOOOOOO-OOOOOoooooooo . . . The skeletons join us, and their rattling bones add much to the sound effects. The tempo increases. The dance goes on, becoming wilder with each passing hour, and we never stop until the rooster crows at dawn. Only then do we fade away in the morning mist. I ask you, friend witch, how's that for scary?
WITCH:	Pretty good, I agree, but not quite good enough. We've completed this list, and *I* win.
GHOST:	No, *I* win. There's no doubt in my mind that I'm much scarier than you.
WITCH:	I can see right now that we're never going to settle this argument.
GHOST:	I guess we'll have to leave it up to folks to decide for themselves, because we're right back where we started.
BOTH:	(*face audience, swaying from side to side*)
	On the night of Halloween Lots of witches and ghosts are seen.
WITCH:	I'm a witch,
GHOST:	and I'm a ghost.
BOTH:	Who is the one that scares you most?
WITCH:	Shall we dance?
GHOST:	(*bows*) Delighted, I'm sure. (*They dance a rousing old-fashioned jitterbug. . . . They bow and exit on opposite sides, the witch returning to get the list*)

Witches and Ghosts

Production notes

PUPPETS:

Both of the characters should be hand-action puppets. The witch should be appropriately homely with a long hooked nose and jutting chin, her appearance matching her own description—all black clothing and pointed hat with brim covering stringy hair. One problem with black costumes is that they don't show up well against a black scrim backdrop. To remedy this, the "rusty stains" mentioned by the witch could be strategically added. This would help to make the witch more visible. The ghost should be entirely white with a round head and black ovals for features. Since this puppet doesn't have to manipulate props, the body part should fit loosely.

SETTING:

Because the play is mostly dialogue, it is not so important that the puppeteers see through the backdrop. Therefore, an additional backdrop—dark blue with a big orange moon—would be a nice touch, and the witch's costume would stand out better. No prop stage is needed.

PROPS:

The only prop is the list, which should be fairly large. It should have a heading, *Scary Qualities* and these should be simply listed—appearance, voice, etc.—in writing large enough for the audience to read (if old enough).

TAPING:

No special sound effects are needed. In this play the voices are especially important to establish convincing characters. The witch's voice should be rasping, and she should be able to screech and cackle as required. The ghost should speak slowly in a low register voice and be able to moan convincingly. Halloween music can be used to introduce the play or (even more effective) spooky Halloween noises. Music used for the closing dance should be bouncy and should fade away after half a minute.

ACTION: The action requires minimal rehearsal. One puppeteer plays each part, and either can operate the tape player. Once on stage the ghost remains till the end, moving only as the dialogue suggests. The witch exits only once, returning immediately with the list, which is then taped to the side curtain (or frame) of the puppet stage. Since stage business is minimal, any movement called for in the script should be exaggerated.

TIME: 11 $^1/_2$ minutes. Allow extra time for introductory music or sound effects and for concluding dance music.

THE THANKSGIVING BEAR

CHARACTERS	PROPS
NARRATOR	TURKEY
BEAR	PIE
FOX	BASKET
RACCOON	
RABBIT	

NARRATOR: Once upon a time there was a jolly old bear who lived in a cave in a deep brown woods. He was a hospitable fellow whose special joy was to entertain his friends. All summer long he had picnics and cookouts. But that time is long past. Now there's a chill in the air.

BEAR: (*enters*) Brrrrrr, it's really cold outside. I can't seem to stop shivering. . . . That must mean it's time for my long winter nap. As my dear mother told me when I was no bigger than your average regulation teddy bear, "When winter comes, you, my son, must hibernate." . . .I love that word. Hibernate. . . . Hibernate. . . . HI-BER-NATE! (*asks audience*) Hey, you out there, let's hear you say it. HI-BER-NATE. . . . HI-BER-NATE. . . . HI-BER-NATE. . . . Very good! I'll bet you already know that hibernate is just a fancy word that means I sleep all winter. . . . But first my favorite holiday is coming up. Thanksgiving! It's time for me to start planning the dinner, and I guess I'd better remind my friends that I'm expecting them as usual. Rabbit's house is right around the corner. I'll

	invite her first. (*crosses stage and calls*) Rabbit, are you home?
RABBIT:	(*enters*) Oh, hello, Bear. What's new?
BEAR:	I just stopped by to remind you that Thanksgiving is coming up soon, so I'll be expecting you to come to my place as usual.
RABBIT:	Oh, dear. I'm really sorry, Bear, but I can't come this year.
BEAR:	Can't come? But you always come to my house on Thanksgiving.
RABBIT:	I know I have in years past, but this year my relatives invited me. We haven't had a get-together for a long time, and, as you know, I come from a *very* large family. Brothers, sisters, cousins by the dozen, not to mention Ma, Pa, plus oodles of aunts and uncles.
BEAR:	Yes, I know, and you're lucky to have such a wonderful, supersized family, but my party won't be the same without you.
RABBIT:	I am truly sorry, Bear. Maybe next year.
BEAR:	All right, I hope so. Well, good-bye, Rabbit.
RABBIT:	Good-bye, Bear. (*exits*)
BEAR:	Well, I'll stop in at Raccoon's hollow tree. It's not far. (*crosses stage and calls*) Raccoon, are you home?
RACCOON:	(*enters*) Hello, Bear, are you getting ready for your winter sleep?
BEAR:	Yes, that's coming up soon. But first, Thanksgiving is just a few days away, and I'm inviting you to come to my house for dinner as usual.
RACCOON:	Oh, sorry, Bear, not this year.
BEAR:	But I was expecting you. You are such a good eater, Raccoon, that it's a pleasure to cook for you.

RACCOON:	That's just the trouble. I've been too good an eater for too long a time, and now I have to go on a diet.
BEAR:	A diet? Not on Thanksgiving surely. That's awful.
RACCOON:	I couldn't agree more, but it's doctor's orders. So while you're enjoying your turkey, plus all the trimmings, I'll be here with a tiny bit of fish and a salad with no dressing.
BEAR:	Oh, that's too bad, Raccoon. Maybe next year will be different. Well, I'd better be on my way. Good-bye. I guess I won't see you again until spring.
RACCOON:	I guess not. Good-bye till then, Bear. I hope you have a good sleep. (*exits*)
BEAR:	(*addresses audience*) This is a fine state of affairs. It looks as if I might be cooking for two this year. Surely Fox will come to my house for Thanksgiving dinner. Well, there's no time like the present to find out. Luckily fox's den is nearby. (*crosses stage and calls*) Fox, Fox, are you at home?
FOX:	Why, hello, Bear. How are you today?
BEAR:	Well, I feel all right, but I'm upset, because I've just been to see Rabbit and Raccoon, and do you know what they told me?
FOX:	No, what did they tell you?
BEAR:	They said that they weren't coming to my house for Thanksgiving dinner this year. Can you believe that? Both of them refused my invitation, and they should know that I would be expecting them, as usual.
FOX:	Uh-oh.
BEAR:	What's the matter, Fox. Please don't tell me that you won't be coming either.
FOX:	I'm sorry, Bear, but I promised myself that I wouldn't have dinner at your house again until you come to my house to eat. I've been to your place ten times in a row, and you haven't been

here at all. So that's why I promised myself no more meals at Bear's this year.

BEAR: But it's Thanksgiving. You have always come to my house on Thanksgiving. It's become a tradition. That's a silly promise you made yourself.

FOX: Silly or not, a promise is a promise. Surely you wouldn't want me to break a promise, not even one that I've made to myself.

BEAR: I guess not, but since Rabbit and Raccoon aren't coming either, Thanksgiving is going to be awful, just awful. Oh, I'm so depressed.

FOX: Bear, I'm sorry, really I am. I'd ask you to come here, but I'm right in the middle of my fall housecleaning, and my den is a mess. We couldn't even sit down in all the clutter.

BEAR: (*sighs*) That's all right. I understand.

FOX: Now come on, Bear. Cheer up! You're the best cook I know, and besides being the best cook, you're also the best eater. You can certainly polish off that whole Thanksgiving feast yourself.

BEAR: No, I certainly won't be cooking a holiday dinner this year. It just wouldn't be the same since there will be no one to share it with. I'll probably eat a peanut butter sandwich, and than I'll settle down to hibernate. Good-bye, Fox.

FOX: Good-bye, Bear. I'll see you next spring. (*exits*)

NARRATOR: (*bear follows directions*) Poor Bear. He trudged back to his cave. Thanksgiving, which had always been his favorite holiday, no longer seemed special. He settled down for a short nap. After all, it doesn't take much time to make a peanut butter sandwich. . . . On Thursday afternoon he roused himself.

BEAR: (*yawning*) Well, it's time for my Thanksgiving dinner. Since no one else is here to share it, I'm certainly not expecting to enjoy myself. A sandwich will be enough. I'm sure I have a jar of peanut butter somewhere and a slice or two of dried-up bread. If I'm lucky, I may find a drop of honey or perhaps a tiny scrape of jelly stuck to the bottom of a jar. (*whimpers*) I guess I should be grateful for that much. Well, that's enough of feeling sorry for myself. I'll look and see what I can find. (*searches*) . . . What' that? I hear noises outside. . . . Who's there? Who's there and what do you want?

FOX: (*enters with turkey and puts it down*) Surprise, Bear! I brought a turkey cooked just the way you like it.

RACCOON: (*enters with pie and puts it down*) And I brought a pumpkin pie. I don't think it is quite as good as what you would have made, but it will do all the same.

RABBIT: (*enters with basket and puts it down*) And I, being a vegetarian, brought cranberries and salad. Happy Thanksgiving, Bear!

BEAR: I-I-I don't know what to say.

RABBIT: Bear, my friend, you have entertained us at so many Thanksgiving dinners. This year we decided that we would do the work and that you would be the guest. Are you surprised?

BEAR: Surprised? I am overwhelmed.

RACCOON: In that case, what are we waiting for? Let's eat. As you all know, I have a wonderful appetite.

BEAR: Wait! First we must all remember that this is a time to give thanks. (*turning to each friend*) Fox. . . . Raccoon. . . . Rabbit. . . . I want you to know that I am grateful for the food you brought today. I know everything will be delicious. But most of all I am thankful for such wonderful friends. Happy Thanksgiving to you all.

OTHERS: Happy Thanksgiving, Bear.

The Thanksgiving Bear

Production notes

PUPPETS: Bear, since he has the biggest speaking part, should be a mouth-action puppet. The others may be either hand- or mouth-action, because they can believably carry their props in either mouths or paws.

SETTING: The woodsy setting is imaginary, but there must be some kind of prop stage, either permanent or temporary, so that the animals can put down their food offerings.

PROPS: Unless something resembling a turkey can be come by easily, a covered dish or pan may be substituted. Children will accept that a turkey is inside. The pumpkin pie could be a small foil tart pan, and if a suitable basket cannot be found, one could be made from brown construction paper or corrugated cardboard.

TAPING: No special sound effects are needed, but the voices should vary in pitch, Bear's being lowest and Rabbit's highest. The pauses allowing for audience participation at the beginning of the play should be carefully observed.

ACTION: The puppeteer on the right should be Bear and Rabbit, and the puppeteer on the left should be Raccoon and Fox. Either may operate the tape player. Bear should make his entrance from the right, his cave home. Once onstage, he never exits, crossing the stage back and forth to each animal's house in turn. Therefore, Rabbit makes her initial entrance and exit at left, Raccoon at right, and Fox at left, after which Bear returns home (at right) for his final actions, all in view of the audience. When the animals make their last entrances with the food, they should come from the left.

TIME: 10 minutes. Allow extra time for introductory music.

THE BUSY SANTA

CHARACTERS

NARRATOR

MRS. CLAUS
POPPINS, AN ELF
SANTA
SNOWMAN

PROPS

BASKET OF FOOD
(COVERED)
LIST
PIPE

NARRATOR: Here at the North Pole life is hectic in December, but the week before Christmas is the busiest of all. Now the front door of Santa's house opens, and here comes Mrs. Claus. She does *not* look happy.

MRS. CLAUS: (*enters and calls*) Santa! Santa! It's dinnertime. . . . Santa Claus! . . .Oh, where is that man? I sent Poppins to the workshop ten minutes ago to remind Santa that dinner would be ready at six sharp. Maybe the naughty elf forgot. . . (*calls*) Poppins! Poppins!

POPPINS: (*enters*) Here I am, Mrs. Claus. Did you want me?

MRS. CLAUS: Yes, Poppins. I sent you to the workshop ten minutes ago to tell Santa that his dinner would be ready at six. Shame on you for forgetting.

POPPINS: But, Mrs. Claus, I didn't forget. I told him, really I did.

MRS. CLAUS: All right, I believe you. But where is he?

POPPINS: He said he'd be right along. Do you want me to go back and see what happened?

83

MRS. CLAUS:	Yes. And if he's still there, I want you to drag him here, by his nose, if necessary.
POPPINS:	All right, Mrs. Claus. You can depend on me. (*exits*)
MRS. CLAUS:	I shouldn't have been cross with Poppins. He's always been a good little elf. But I hate to have my fine dinner ruined. . . . (*looks offstage*) I think I see them coming. . . . (*clock chimes six*)
POPPINS:	(*enters pulling Santa by the nose*) Well, Mrs. Claus, here he is, as ordered.
MRS. CLAUS:	Santa, shame on you! Do you know what time it is?
SANTA:	Yes, my dear, I heard the clock strike six.
MRS. CLAUS:	Well, you wouldn't have heard the clock if Poppins hadn't dragged you here. You are certainly old enough to know that six o'clock is dinnertime.
SANTA:	Yes, my dear, and I'm sorry, truly I am. But at this time of year we're so busy that I hardly have time to think of food.
MRS. CLAUS:	Well, you're here now, and I'm going to feed you a good hot meal. It's on the table waiting, so come in and eat. (*exits*)
SANTA:	Yes, dear. (*exits*)
POPPINS:	I know that Santa doesn't want to upset Mrs. Claus, but he hates to leave the workshop in late December. I'll bet that instead of enjoying her superior cooking he's gobbling his dinner in one, two, three bites. Yes, I'm afraid I'm right. Here he comes already.
SANTA:	(*enters and turns to shout*) Thank you, my dear. Your food was delicious, as usual. . . . (*burps*) Oops! Please excuse me. In late December my digestion is not as it should be. Well, back to the workshop. (*exits*)

POPPINS: Poor Santa, I know he loves his wife's cooking, even though he's much too busy to enjoy it now. And poor Mrs. Claus, she's as mad as a soggy reindeer after a fast thaw. But I'd better get back to the workshop, too. (*exits*)

MRS. CLAUS: (*enters*) I'm disgusted. I plan all the meals for the elves' dining room, three shifts a day at this time of year, and I try my best to see that Santa has a decent diet. And what thanks do I get? Santa just doesn't realize that this is my busiest time of year, too. No one appreciates me.

SNOWMAN: (*talks from offstage*) You know that's not true. Everyone appreciates you, Santa most of all.

MRS. CLAUS: (*looking about*) Who's there? I hear a voice, but I don't see anyone.

SNOWMAN: (*enters*) I'm the one you hear, Mrs. Claus.

MRS. CLAUS: Why, it's the snowman from the front yard!

SNOWMAN: Right you are.

MRS. CLAUS: I'm amazed! I didn't know you could move about, and I certainly never guessed that you could talk.

SNOWMAN: Life is full of surprises, Mrs. Claus. I'll admit that usually I just stand in the yard looking handsome. Late at night, though, after you're asleep, I exercise a bit, and sometimes I even sing a few bars of a Christmas carol. . . .

(*sings*) Deck the halls with boughs of holly,
Fa la la la la, la la la la. . . .

Of course overdoing that could be dangerous to my health, because singing carols makes me feel warm and cozy. If I get *too* warm and cozy, it's good-bye, Mr. Snowman—hello, Mr. Puddle.

MRS. CLAUS: Oh, I see what you mean. Well, we certainly wouldn't want you to melt. What I don't understand is why you decided to talk to me now.

SNOWMAN: I couldn't bear for you to be so upset. And standing here as I do, I have a lot of time to think. When I saw Santa being dragged up here—by his nose yet—I got an idea. It just may solve your problems.

MRS. CLAUS: Breakfast is no problem, because Santa eats here before he leaves, and he always takes a sandwich for lunch. But dinner is something else, so please tell me your idea. I'll listen to any suggestions you have. A good meal at night is so important.

SNOWMAN: Very well then. Have you ever heard of "Meals on Wheels"?

MRS. CLAUS: Why, yes. Yes, I have. Those are hot, nourishing meals delivered to shut-ins. But I don't know what you're getting at. We don't have any shut-ins here. Everyone is in perfect health, thank goodness. And we certainly don't need any meals delivered, not as long as I can cook.

SNOWMAN: Please, Mrs. Claus, let me finish. You can continue to cook all of Santa's meals, but instead of coming here to the house, Santa can stay at the workshop and eat when his dinner is delivered. Then he'll be able to eat slowly and enjoy it more. He can even chew his food instead of swallowing huge chunks of meat and potatoes whole. That way he can keep an eye on toy production and check the jobs off his list as they get done.

MRS. CLAUS: But I'll miss Santa's company at dinnertime.

SNOWMAN: Mrs. Claus, it will only be for a few more days. After Christmas, things will be different.

MRS. CLAUS: Mr. Snowman, you're right. I'll follow your suggestion exactly, except we won't need wheels. I'll deliver the hot meals myself. That way I can say hello to Santa and *bon appétit!*

SNOWMAN: Good, Mrs. Claus. I'm pleased that I could help. Also, I'm glad I broke my vow never to walk and

	talk when someone's around. Now I must return to the front yard.
MRS. CLAUS:	May I give you a little hug first?
SNOWMAN:	I'd be delighted! But just a little one. I'm already melting a bit around the edges. (*they hug*)
MRS. CLAUS:	Good-bye, Mr. Snowman, and thanks.
SNOWMAN:	GOOD-bye, Mrs. Claus. (*waves and exits*)
MRS. CLAUS:	I feel so much happier, but now I must rush in to plan especially delicious meals for these last few days before Christmas.
NARRATOR:	So Mrs. Claus set to work, and let me tell you, the results were scrumptious. (*as each meal is described Mrs. Claus crosses stage with covered basket*) On December 22 Mrs. Claus made beef Stroganoff and Caesar salad with cherry pie à la mode for dessert. . . . On December 23 she cooked spaghetti and meatballs with garlic bread, and for dessert strawberry shortcake with whipped cream. . . . And on December 24, Christmas Eve, she made chicken and dumplings, because this was Santa's favorite meal. Knowing he'd be outside in the cold all night, she brought two desserts, hot apple pie with cheese and chocolate layer cake with nuts on top. . . .
MRS. CLAUS:	(*enters*) Well, my husband is about to go. His sleigh is loaded and the reindeer hitched up and ready. . . . (*calls*) Good-bye. . . . Good-bye, Santa! (*waves*)
SANTA:	(*calls from offstage*) Good-bye . . . Good-bye. . . . Ho-ho-ho!
SNOWMAN:	(*enters*) I'm happy to see that my plan worked.
MRS. CLAUS:	Yes, it worked beautifully, and I'm ever so grateful. Now I'd like to do something nice for you. What would you like?

SNOWMAN:	Nothing that I can think of. Since I'm a snowman, I certainly can't enjoy your hot meals. Just wish me a merry Christmas.
MRS. CLAUS:	That I'll do. Merry Christmas, dear Mr. Snowman.
SNOWMAN:	And the same to you, Mrs. Claus. Good-bye. (*they exit in opposite directions*)
NARRATOR:	The long night passed, and in the morning, his work done, Santa returned home, tired but happy. He had delivered everything on his long list.
SANTA:	(*enters carrying list*) I'm home! I'm home!
MRS. CLAUS:	(*enters*) I'm so glad to see you, my dear. (*they hug*) . . . But before I feed you my special eggs Benedict, there's something I must do. . . . (*calls*) Poppins! Poppins!
POPPINS:	Yes, Mrs. Claus, what can I do for you?
MRS. CLAUS:	I have an errand for you. Wait here just a minute. (*exits and returns with pipe*) Please take this to the snowman in the front yard. Tell him it's a Christmas present from me, because he's very special, and every snowman should have a pipe.
POPPINS:	(*taking pipe*) All right, Mrs. Claus. Will do. (*exits*)
MRS. CLAUS:	Before we go inside, Santa, please tell me something. Why did you bring that list home with you?
SANTA:	I wanted to show you that every single thing was crossed off. And what better to kindle that cozy fire, that I'm going to light in the fireplace before we have our Christmas breakfast?
MRS. CLAUS:	That's a beautiful idea, Santa. (*they hug*) Let's go in now. Breakfast is on the table.
SANTA:	I plan to eat it slowly, and I'm going to enjoy every bite. (*they exit*)

The Busy Santa

Production notes

PUPPETS: All of the puppets should be hand-action, and their appearance should conform to the children's conception of the characters portrayed. Like Santa, Mrs. Claus should wear red, and glasses and white hair would be fitting. Some padding for Santa and the snowman would be appropriate, and the latter should have a hat and scarf.

SETTING: Nothing visual is needed to indicate that all of the action takes place right outside Santa's house, and no prop stage is necessary.

PROPS: If an appropriate basket cannot be found, one could be made of brown construction paper or corrugated cardboard, or any kind of small container covered with a cloth could be used, or even a little box. Santa's list could be made from cash register tape with the items checked and crossed off so that the audience can see. The snowman's pipe could be a real one, or one could be made from a lollipop stick and the cap from a small bottle.

TAPING: The only sound effect is the chiming of the clock, which can be accomplished by tapping a glass of water with a spoon. Santa should have a deep, hearty voice, and the snowman's should be slightly higher. Since Mrs. Claus and Poppins converse, their voices should be as different as possible, Mrs. Claus's being higher in pitch. The narrator can be any good reader.

ACTION: The puppeteer on the right should be Mrs. Claus
            and the snowman. The puppeteer on the left
            should be Poppins and Santa. Either may operate
            the tape player. Mrs. Claus should always enter
            from the right, the location of the house. She
            should always exit right, too, except for the three
            trips to Santa's workshop when she crosses the
            stage and exits left. Her return to the house should
            not be staged, and she never releases the basket as
            the puppeteer returns her (out of audience vision)
            for the next trip as the narrator is describing the
            menu. The other characters always enter and exit
            left, the yard/workshop direction, excepting the
            two times when Santa enters his house with Mrs.
            Claus.

TIME: 11 minutes. Allow extra time for introductory
            music.

SILVIE THE SUBSTITUTE REINDEER

CHARACTERS

SANTA
MRS. CLAUS
JIGGS, AN ELF
SILVIE, A REINDEER

PROP

BLANKET

SANTA: (*enters*) I can't believe it. The sleigh is packed, ready to go. . . . I can't believe it.

MRS. CLAUS: (*enters*) Are you talking to me, Santa?

SANTA: No, Mrs. Claus, I was talking to myself.

MRS. CLAUS: Some people might say that's a sign of old age. Of course, I know better than that. You're as sharp as ever, Santa. So, now that I'm here, you can talk to me. I think I heard you say that you couldn't believe something. What can't you believe?

SANTA: The sleigh is packed, ready to go, and we're two hours ahead of schedule. Even Jiggs says we're ready, and since he's the elf in charge, it must be true. Nothing has gone wrong this year. I can't believe it.

MRS. CLAUS: My goodness, I can hardly believe that myself. Are you sure you haven't forgotten something?

SANTA: I'm positive. I've not only checked my list twice, but three times. All the toys and presents are in the sleigh, and with two hours to spare. This has never happened before.

MRS. CLAUS: That's wonderful! Maybe you can get off to an early start.

91

SANTA:	Oh, no, Mrs. Claus. That would never do. I can't deliver any presents until the children are all asleep.
MRS. CLAUS:	Then, speaking of sleep, why don't you take a little nap yourself? You haven't had much time to relax this past week. It would do you good.
SANTA:	But I've never, *ever* taken a nap on Christmas Eve. I don't know . . .
MRS. CLAUS:	You can stretch out on the sofa in the parlor. Wait a minute, and I'll get something to cover you. (*exits*)
SANTA:	I must admit, a short nap might be pleasant. But I still can't believe that everything has gone so well. We have never before been ready two hours early.
MRS. CLAUS:	(*enters with blanket*) Here you are, Santa, and you needn't worry. I'll wake you in plenty of time. Now, go lie down, and I'll tuck you in.
SANTA:	All right, Mrs. Claus. I'm going. (*turns to leave*)
JIGGS:	(*enters*) Santa! Santa! We have a problem.
SANTA:	Why, Jiggs, what's wrong?
JIGGS:	I'm so sorry, Santa, but one of the reindeer has taken sick. I hitched up the team for a practice run, and just as they started, Prancer began to sneeze. I can tell he has an awful cold. He insists on going anyway, but that's not a good idea at all.
SANTA:	Oh, no. If he's sick, he should stay here.
JIGGS:	He certainly should. Every time he sneezes, the sleigh jerks. During the practice run, a doll popped right out of your pack, which we couldn't quite close, because it's an extra big load this year.
SANTA:	Well, we can't have our toys popping out. The sleigh must run smoothly, so you'll have to find a substitute for Prancer.

JIGGS:	(*whimpering*) Oooooh, that's the worst of it. I thought everything was all set to go, so I told the other reindeer that they could leave to join the herd. All of the big, strong ones are long gone.
SANTA:	But we'll need a full team with such a heavy load. Send out an emergency call, and hurry.
JIGGS:	All right, Santa, I'll do my best. (*exits*)
MRS. CLAUS:	Poor Santa. You won't get a nap after all.
SANTA:	That's the least of my worries. I knew it was too good to be true, being ready so early. I just hope that Jiggs finds me a good substitute for Prancer.
MRS. CLAUS:	Well, I guess you won't be needing this blanket, so I'll put it away. (*exits with blanket*)
SILVIE:	(*enters*) Santa! Santa Claus! I must talk to you.
SANTA:	Oh, it's a reindeer! That's just what I need most, but I had hoped for something larger. . . . Hello, my dear, what can I do for you?
SILVIE:	It's not what *you* can do for *me*. It's what *I* can do for *you*.
SANTA:	Whatever do you mean?
SILVIE:	I'm here to take Prancer's place.
SANTA:	Take Prancer's place? Ho-ho-ho! This little reindeer has a sense of humor.
SILVIE:	Please don't ho-ho-ho at me, Santa. I am not joking. That elf is looking everywhere for a sub, but he won't find anyone better. I am ready, willing, and able to do the job, and now you're laughing at me.
SANTA:	There, there. I didn't mean to hurt your feelings. You are a pretty little reindeer, one of the prettiest I've seen, in fact. But good looks are not what I need. Prancer is big and strong, and I need a big, strong reindeer to take his place.

SILVIE: A big, strong *boy* reindeer?

SANTA: Exactly! I'm glad you understand.

SILVIE: But, Santa, I don't understand. I may not be as big as Prancer, but I am strong. All of the deer on your team are boys, and that's not fair. Why, in spite of his feminine name, I happen to know that even Vixen is a boy reindeer. We girls deserve a chance, too.

SANTA: My goodness! In all the years I've been driving my sleigh, I never thought of having a lady reindeer on my team.

SILVIE: Santa Claus, surely you think girls are as good as boys. All of the little girls in the world would be disappointed to think that you really like boys better.

SANTA: And that wouldn't be true. I think little girls are every bit as good as little boys, and often much better behaved.

SILVIE: Then you should be fair and give me a chance to join your team tonight.

SANTA: If you are as strong as you are spunky, I might take you up on your offer. Tell me, my dear, what is your name?

SILVIE: My name is Silver Bell. Doesn't that have a Christmasy ring to it?

SANTA: (*laughs*) You *do* have a sense of humor. Silver Bell does indeed have a Christmasy ring.

SILVIE: But it's a bit formal, so most folks call me Silvie.

SANTA: Silvie it is then! Very well, Silvie, are you sure you want to try this? Being hitched to a sleigh is much harder than running free.

SILVIE: I have pulled sleds for the elves many times. I'm sure I can do my share of the work pulling your sleigh.

SANTA:	We would have to give you a tryout. That's twice around the house.
SILVIE:	I'm ready.
JIGGS:	(*enters panting*) Santa . . . I haven't found a new reindeer yet . . . but I'm sending a scout to look for the herd. I'm sure any minute I'll find a fill-in for Prancer.
SANTA:	There's no need to worry. Silvie here has volunteered for the job.
JIGGS:	But she . . . she . . . she is a girl reindeer. Surely you wouldn't consider her.
SANTA:	She has convinced me that she can do the work, and she's ready to take the test. So, hitch her up for a trial run with the team. Twice around the house should tell the tale.
JIGGS:	All right, Santa, if you say so. Come with me, Silvie, and we'll see what happens. (*exits*)
SILVIE:	I'm coming. (*exits*)
MRS. CLAUS:	(*enters*) I just saw Jiggs leaving with Silver Bell. What's up?
SANTA:	Oh, do you know little Silvie?
MRS. CLAUS:	Goodness, yes. Usually she's pulling a sledful of elves. She's a hard worker, and very strong for her size. But why was she here?
SANTA:	Silvie wants to take Prancer's place on the team. What do you think of that?
MRS. CLAUS:	I never thought you would consider a lady reindeer, but I don't know why not. It's a wonderful idea.
SANTA:	Jiggs has hitched her to the sleigh for a trial run with the others. Twice around the house, and we'll know how she performs. . . . Oh, here comes Jiggs now, all smiles.

JIGGS:	(*enters*) Santa, I'm so relieved. Silvie did a fine job, every bit as good as Prancer has done in the past. Our worries are over.
SANTA:	That's wonderful news.
MRS. CLAUS:	And there's still enough time for you to take a short nap, Santa.
SANTA:	No, I'm not going to do that after all. Now that I think about it, taking a nap on Christmas Eve doesn't seem natural. I'm going out to do some last minute checking myself and also to congratulate Silvie on her good work. (*exits*)
JIGGS:	All of this is very strange somehow. I never thought I'd see the day when a girl reindeer would be pulling Santa's sleigh.
MRS. CLAUS:	I never did either, but times are changing.
JIGGS:	I suppose next that lady elves will be wanting jobs in Santa's workshop.
MRS. CLAUS:	And what would be wrong with that?
JIGGS:	Oh, nothing, nothing at all, Mrs. Claus.
MRS. CLAUS:	I hope you think that girls are as capable as boys.
JIGGS:	Yes, yes, yes. Of course, I do. It's just so different from what I'm used to.
MRS. CLAUS:	And it's about time, I say.
JIGGS:	I suppose you're right.
MRS. CLAUS:	What would you say if I told you that next year *I* might drive the sleigh?
JIGGS:	Why . . . why . . . uh . . . uh . . .
MRS. CLAUS:	(*laughs*) Don't look so shocked. I was teasing you, Jiggs. I don't want to take Santa's job away. . . . Of course, if he got a terrible cold like Prancer's, I might have to fill in.

JIGGS: And I'm sure you would do it very well, too, very well indeed. Yes, yes, yes.

MRS. CLAUS: To tell the truth, I hope I never have to. Being out all night in the cold doesn't appeal to me at all. Oh, here comes Santa.

SANTA: (*enters*) Everything checks out perfectly. It's still a bit early, but I think I'll start off now. Good-bye, Jiggs, my good friend. (*they shake hands*)

JIGGS: Good-bye, Santa.

SANTA: Good-bye, Mrs. Claus. I'll see you at dawn. (*hugs her and exits*)

MRS. CLAUS: (*calling after him and waving*) Good-bye, Santa. Have a safe journey. . . . Jiggs, I'm sure all will go well now, with Silver Bell on the team.

JIGGS: Yes, I have to agree. Silvie, the substitute reindeer, has truly saved the day.

Silvie the Substitute Reindeer

Production notes

PUPPETS: Santa, Mrs. Claus, and Jiggs should be hand-action puppets. Santa and Mrs. Claus should be in red costumes, conforming to popular conception of the characters they represent. Silvie should be a mouth-action puppet. Since female reindeer are antlered, she should have horns. A collar with one or more small sleigh bells would be appropriate.

SETTING: The exact scene, which remains the same throughout, is not specified, but it is somewhere in Santa's house. No prop stage is necessary.

PROPS: Any small piece of cloth could be used for the blanket, which is the only prop.

TAPING: No sound effects are needed for this play. Of the two male voices, Santa's should be the deeper. Since the two female characters never converse, difference in pitch is not essential, but the voice quality should be different.

ACTION: The puppeteer on the right should operate the tape player and be Mrs. Claus and Silvie. The puppeteer on the left should be Santa and Jiggs. The action is simple to remember. Mrs. Claus's entrances and exits are all to the right, and the other characters enter and exit left.

TIME: 11 minutes. Allow extra time for introductory music.

Five Little Snowmen

CHARACTERS

NARRATOR
5 SNOWMEN

(Snowmen enter from below, follow narrator's description of the action, and disappear, one by one)

NARRATOR: Five little snowmen all in a row,
Dancing, dancing, watch them go!
One danced too close to the barnyard door.
He danced inside, so then there were four. . . .
Four little snowmen were playing hard,
Jumping, jumping in the yard.
One jumped and hit the limb of a tree.
He fell down, so then there were three. . . .
Three little snowmen skipped through the snow,
Skipping, skipping to and fro.
Not turning as he was supposed to do,
One skipped away, so then there were two. . . .
Two little snowmen began to spin around,
Spinning, spinning across the snowy ground.
One spun so fast, because it was fun,
That he spun away completely, so then there was
   one. . . .
One little snowman stood all alone,
Standing, standing as the warm sun shone.
He stood so long in the noonday sun
That he melted away, and then there was
   none. . . .

But don't be sad, 'cause I'm telling you
That's what all little snowmen do.
And here are the puppet snowmen now
To say good-bye and take a bow. . . .
(*snowmen sink from sight*)

Five Little Snowmen

Production notes

PUPPETS: These should be stick puppets. A snowman pup-
            pet can easily be made from foam balls, two for the
            body and a smaller one for the head with thin
            slices cut off to allow flat surfaces for gluing. Eyes,
            nose, mouth, and buttons can be made of black
            felt. A foot of thin dowel sharpened in a pencil
            sharpener can be blackened with a felt marker (the
            better to blend with the background curtain) and
            inserted into the body.

TAPING: The narrator should recite slowly and with feel-
            ing. No special sound effects are needed, but
            several bars of music—bells, guitar, or a toy
            xylophone would be effective—could be inserted
            briefly after each snowman exits, reprising intro-
            ductory music.

ACTION: The puppeteer on the left should operate the tape
            player so that the one on the right can manage
            three snowmen until the first exit. The snowmen
            should rise in a line, and the puppeteers then
            follow the narrator's lead, exiting alternately right
            and left. By the time spinning is required, only
            two snowmen are left, and the sticks can be rolled
            between the puppeteer's hands.

TIME: 2 minutes. Allow extra time for music.

THE LOOSE TOOTH

CHARACTERS

BOY
MOTHER
TOOTH FAIRY

PROPS

PIECE OF STRING
TOOTH
PILLOW
COIN
APPLE

BOY:	(*enters crying*) Mom! . . . Mom! . . . (*sobs and thrashes about*)
MOTHER:	(*enters*) Oh, my poor child! Are you hurt?
BOY:	No!
MOTHER:	Well, what's wrong then?
BOY:	Something awful. (*sobs and thrashes*)
MOTHER:	There, there. Come here and let me give you a big hug. (*dramatic hugs and pats*) . . . Now do you feel better?
BOY:	No!
MOTHER:	Did you do something naughty in school so that Ms. Murgatroyd had to make you sit in the corner?
BOY:	No!
MOTHER:	Oh, I know! You had a fight with your best friend, Mary Martha McGillicuddy.
BOY:	No, nothing like that.

MOTHER:	Aha! I'll bet you got into my cookie jar again and broke it.
BOY:	No! No! No!
MOTHER:	All right, I give up. What happened?
BOY:	Well, I was just walking along minding my own business and being very good the way I always am . . .
MOTHER:	Ha-ha! *Very* good, the way you always are? That *is* a funny joke. Tell me more.
BOY:	Well, as I said before you so rudely interrupted—and you did tell me that interrupting was rude, didn't you—or at least that's what I seem to remember your saying.
MOTHER:	Yes, I admit I probably said that, but now you are interrupting yourself.
BOY:	Oh, yes, I guess I am. Maybe I'd better start all over from the beginning. . . . I was just walking along, minding my own business *and* being very good the way I always am . . .
MOTHER:	Y-e-ss, go on. . . .
BOY:	. . . and I was eating an apple. Eating an apple *is* on the approved list of activities for people my age, right?
MOTHER:	Yes, eating an apple is a good thing to do.
BOY:	But then something awful happened.
MOTHER:	Oh, dear! I'll bet there was a wiggly, slimy brown worm in the apple, and you swallowed it.
BOY:	No, a wiggly, slimy brown worm might taste good. What happened was something worse, much, much worse. Please, just look inside my mouth.
MOTHER:	(*looks*) I can't see anything wrong.

BOY:	It's this tooth right in front. It's all funny and wobbly.
MOTHER:	(*laughing*) Oh, is that all?
BOY:	*All?* Is that *all*, she says! If this tooth gets any looser, it might fall out!
MOTHER:	You're right. I'm sure it will fall out, and then, sooner or later, so will your other teeth.
BOY:	Oh, what am I going to do?
MOTHER:	(*laughs*) Don't worry. Everything will be all right.
BOY:	Don't laugh. It's not funny. I don't want to be like my great-granny with no teeth at all.
MOTHER:	I told you not to worry. All boys and girls lose their baby teeth.
BOY:	They do?
MOTHER:	Yes, and every time a tooth comes out, a big, beautiful new one will grow in to take its place.
BOY:	Well, that makes me feel better.
MOTHER:	Wait here just a minute. I'll get some thread. . . . (*exits and returns with a piece of string*) Here, let's tie this around your loose tooth, and I'll yank it right out. . . .
BOY:	(*covers mouth*) Oh, no!
MOTHER:	(*patiently*) . . . Or we could tie the thread around your tooth and attach the other end to a doorknob, and then, when someone opens the door very fast, like this . . . (*motions*)
BOY:	(*backs away*) No, no. That would hurt.
MOTHER:	I give up. We'll just wait until it falls out by itself. Meanwhile, I have work to do. I'll see you later. (*exits*)
BOY:	Maybe if I'm very careful my tooth won't fall out at all. I'm sure about one thing though. I'm

certainly not going to let someone pull it out with a piece of thread. I'll forget about it for now and run out to play. . . . (*exits briefly and reenters*) . . .Oh, I'm glad to be out here skipping along instead of worrying about my tooth. (*skips*) . . . Oops! . . . (*falls flat*) . . . Oh, I fell right on my poor face. I'd better check my eyes. . . . They're okay. Nose? . . . It's fine. Mouth? . . . Oh, my tooth is gone! I didn't need that old thread on the doorknob after all. I must look for it so that I can show Mom. (*searches frantically*) Oh, where is it? I hope it's not lost. Ah, here it is! (*picks up tooth, exits, and reenters immediately*) . . . Mom! Mom! Come here a minute.

MOTHER: (*enters*) What's wrong? What's happened to you now?

BOY: I lost my loose baby tooth, but then I found it. Here it is! (*shows tooth*)

MOTHER: It's beautiful! But you don't want to lose it again, so run inside and put it on the kitchen counter where it will be safe.

BOY: All right. (*exits and returns without tooth*) Are you going to save my tooth? Is that why you told me to put it on the kitchen counter?

MOTHER: We'll save it till tonight, and then we'll put it under your pillow.

BOY: Why would we want to do a strange thing like that?

MOTHER: Because, when you're asleep the tooth fairy will come and take it.

BOY: Do you mean that a wicked fairy will steal my tooth? Stealing is a bad thing to do.

MOTHER: The tooth fairy will take your tooth, but she will leave you something nice to take its place.

BOY: Oh, boy! Maybe she'll leave me a candy bar. A candy bar would be a nice thing to get.

MOTHER:	No, I'm sure it won't be a candy bar. The tooth fairy does not approve of candy bars. All that sugar? Never!
BOY:	Maybe she'll leave me a bicycle. I'd love to have a bicycle.
MOTHER:	No, it has to be something small that will fit under your pillow.
BOY:	What nice thing would be small and fit under my pillow?
MOTHER:	Well, when I was your age, the tooth fairy usually left money.
BOY:	Money? That would be fine! I think I'll take a nap now and see what happens.
MOTHER:	A nap? I can't believe my ears. You have never, never, *never* wanted to take a nap, not since you were three years old.
BOY:	Well, I do now. I'm suddenly very sleepy. Can't you see me yawning? (*stretches*) . . . I'm so-o-o sleepy.
MOTHER:	Very well. You can nap right here on the porch.
BOY:	I will. But first I must get my pillow, . . . (*exits and returns with pillow*) . . . and now I must get my tooth. . . . (*exits and returns with tooth, which he puts under pillow*)
MOTHER:	I'll leave you now. Sweet dreams. (*exits*)
BOY:	(*lies down*) This is so comfy. . . (*snores*)

* * * * * * * *

TOOTH FAIRY:	(*enters from above, carrying coin*) Ah, a sleeping child! My magic radar tells me that there's a tooth here for my collection. I must look under his pillow. . . (*looks*) Yes, my radar is always right. There's a tooth here for me. I'll leave this bright new coin for him. . . . There! (*leaves coin*)

... And I'll take this beautiful tooth. (*flies away with tooth*)

* * * * * * * *

BOY: (*sits up*) Time to wake up. (*stretches*) ... Oh-ah-oh! It feels so good to stretch. And now to look under my pillow. (*looks*) Oh, joy! Money! (*picks up coin*) Mom! Mom!

MOTHER: (*enters*) Yes, what is it? Are you finished with your nap already?

BOY: Yes, and look what the tooth fairy left me!

MOTHER: Oh, that's nice. What are you going to do with it?

BOY: Well, now, let's see. . . . Oh, I know! I'm going to buy an apple.

MOTHER: An apple? Well, I must say that I'm surprised. Why are you going to buy an apple?

BOY: Because eating an apple is what made my first tooth loose. If I can make my other teeth loose, then they will soon fall out, too, and I'll be rich, rich, rich! Good-bye for now. I'll be back soon. (*exits with coin*)

MOTHER: (*calls after him*) Good-bye! But there's no need to hurry back. I still have work to do. (*exits with pillow*)

BOY: (*enters with apple to take his bow*)

The Loose Tooth

PUPPETS:
Both the boy and mother must be hand-action puppets in order to carry their props. The tooth fairy, only briefly on stage, could be a small hand-action puppet or a rod puppet seen in silhouette with a pinch clothespin for hands to hold the coin and later the tooth. The rod should be black to match the backdrop. If a hand-action puppet is used, the puppeteer's arm should be black sleeved.

SETTING:
Except for the pillow, no props are set down, so a prop stage is not needed to suggest the porch where most of the play takes place. The pillow, used only briefly, could be rested on the puppet stage frame.

PROPS:
Although the script mentions thread, a piece of string would show up better against the backdrop. The tooth, which can be made of cardboard, should be oversized and have a root so that it will be visible when held by the puppets. A small beanbag would make a good pillow, especially if a prop stage is not used, since its weight would keep it in place. The coin can be a real one. A quarter or half dollar would show up best. The apple, used only during the boy's bow, could be real or fake. A small red ball would work.

TAPING:
Other than the sobs and snores provided by the person taping the boy's part, no sound effects are needed. The boy's voice should have enough range

so that he can emote noisily as the script requires. The mother's voice should be mature and throaty, and the tooth fairy's light. Any music used at the beginning should *not* be reprised during the sleeping intervals that bracket the tooth fairy's visit. A segment of lullaby music overlaid by a few snores would be more effective.

ACTION: The puppeteer on the left should operate the tape player and take the part of the mother. Her entrances and exits are all made from that, the "house," side. The same puppeteer can manipulate the tooth fairy, whose appearance may be made from high up on either side. The puppeteer on the right should be the boy. He enters and exits right except for the errands that take him into the house. His sobbing and thrashing at the play's beginning should be exaggerated. The tooth and coin should not actually be placed under the pillow but into the waiting hand of the puppeteer below audience vision. Likewise, the tooth is handed to the tooth fairy. This will work much better than having the puppets manipulate tiny props on their own.

TIME: 9 $1/2$ minutes. Allow extra time for introductory and iterim music.

THE TALENT SHOW

CHARACTERS

MS. POTTS
WILLY
JODY
RACHEL
LESLIE
TWINS, JERRY AND TERRY
MELODY

PROP

PAINTING

MS. POTTS: (*enters*) Ladies and gentlemen, girls and boys, may I have your attention, *please*? . . . As you know—or at least I *hope* you know—my class at the Happy Day School presents a talent show every year. My children are chock-full of talent, and why not, with me for a teacher? (*laughs*) Today I, Ms. Penelope Potts, will act as your emcee. That's short for *Mizz* of ceremonies. (*laughs*) That way I can keep my eye on the ~~little so-and-so-and-sos. Oops! I~~ *meant* ~~to say on the~~ talented cast of entertainers. Well, let's begin. . . .We will start with a song. Here is Willy McGilly, and I think once you've heard him that you will agree that he is really something special. (*exits*)

WILLY: (*enters, sings, . . . bows, and exits*)

MS. POTTS: (*enters*) Bravo, Willy! In a few years it's the Metropolitan Opera for you. . . . And now, dear people, I ask you, what would a program like ours be without a dramatic recitation? Therefore, I am

thrilled to present Jody Dody with ~~his~~ *her* rendition
of a work by ~~Mr. Isaac Watts. (exits)~~

JODY: *(enters and recites with gestures)*

How doth the little busy bee
  Improve each shining hour,
And gather honey all the day
  From every opening flower!
How skillfully she builds her cell;
  How neat she spreads the wax!
And labours hard to store it well
  With the sweet food she makes.

I hope you all liked my poem. It's supposed to
teach you a real good lesson, but I'm not sure what
that is. *(bows and exits)*

MS. POTTS: *(enters)* Jody, that was worthy of an Oscar. And
now, let me see what treat I have for you next. Ah,
yes, it is something a wee bit unusual. Rachel Roy
is a darling little girl, but she would not—I
repeat, would not—perform. But of course she is
talented, like all of my children. May I present
Rachel Roy with her painting, "Sunrise Over
Grampy's Farm!" *(exits)*

RACHEL: *(enters, displays picture, bows, and exits)*

MS. POTTS: *(enters)* Thank you, Rachel. That was lovely, and
now, . . . *(Rachel reenters, displays picture, bows, and
exits.)* . . . Thank you again, Rachel. Well, to go on,
. . . *(Rachel reenters and remains on stage swinging picture
about.)* . . . Rachel, you've had your turn. Why don't
you take yet another bow and exit for good this
time? Please, everyone, give Rachel a big hand.
(sound of two hands clapping. . . . Rachel bows and exits)
And now, to continue, Leslie Ogletree is next. She
has been taking tap lessons, so now she will dance
for you. He-e-e-re's Leslie. *(exits)*

LESLIE: *(enters, dances, . . . bows, and exits)*

MS. POTTS: (*enters*) Marvelous! Absolutely marvelous! Soon it will be Broadway for Leslie. . . . Next we have a double feature. Twins! Jerry and Terry are new to the school, and (*whispers*) they are very, *very* shy. . . . But, bless their little hearts, they have prepared an act for you. It is my pleasure to present Jerry and Terry Boysenberry. (*exits*)

TWINS: (*enter and recite with appropriate hand motions*)

Pease porridge hot, pease porridge cold,
Pease porridge in the pot nine days old.
Some like it hot, some like it cold,
Some like it in the pot nine days old.

(*Twins bow and exit giggling*)

MS. POTTS: (*enters*) That was wonderful, twins. I'm proud of you. Now for our final act, what could be more appropriate than a song? Melody Moon is going to sing for you. And Melody, who's really a good kid, says if you know the words, you can sing along. You're on, Melody. (*exits*)

MELODY: (*enters, sings, . . . bows, and exits*)

MS. POTTS: (*enters*) Thank you, Melody. That was splendid. . . . Alas, dear people, all good things must end, so our talent show is now over. You have been a wonderful audience. Thank you. Thank you. Thank you. (*bows and exits*)

RACHEL: (*enters once more, displays picture, bows, and exits*)

The Talent Show

PUPPETS: Ms. Potts, Willy, and Melody should be mouth-action puppets since talking or singing is all they are required to do. The others should be hand-action puppets so that they can move according to directions. The twins should be identical, small, and flexible enough to perform the hand-clapping motions associated with the nursery rhyme.

PROP: The picture should be painted with felt-tipped pens on a piece of poster board about eight inches wide with two holes for cord that can be attached to the puppet's hands. It should be simple and bright and suggestive of a rayed sunset.

TAPING: Ms. Potts should speak dramatically and affectedly, showing enthusiasm and annoyance as required. Jody should have a middle-register voice and should speak slowly and solemnly. The twins should have high voices. A soft-shoe rhythm should be used for the dance number, and a minute is enough. Hitting a jar lid with spoons may be done to simulate the taps. Songs chosen should be humorous and not so long that the audience loses interest. The final one should be an old favorite so that the audience can join in. The pauses should be observed during Rachel's repeated appearances, so that the timing will be right.

ACTION: The puppeteer on the right should be Ms. Potts and can operate the tape player. All of Ms. Potts's entrances and exits should be made at the right. The puppeteer on the left should be all the other characters. It is especially important that both twins be manipulated by the same puppeteer so that the clapping motions coordinate. All of these puppets should enter and exit left.

TIME: 7 minutes. With the addition of music for the dance and also possibly at the start, plus the two songs, this show could easily extend to 15 minutes.

CLEVER PETS

CHARACTERS

CHILD
POLLY-PAT, A PARROT
BUSTER, A DOG

PROPS

PARROT PERCH
BOOK

	(*Parrot is on stage*)
CHILD:	(*enters carrying open book in one hand*) This is one great book. It's called *How to Train Your Pet to Do Tricks*, and it just so happens that there is a chapter titled "Teaching Your Parrot to Talk." Polly-Pat is a very nice parrot, and she's certainly pretty, but so far she hasn't said one word. All she does is squawk and whistle. Let's see what the book says. (*reads*) "Repeat a simple phrase several times whenever you pass your parrot's cage or perch." Well, that sounds like a good idea, and I've heard that parrots like the sound of their own names, so I think I'll try something I've said to her before. Here goes. . . . (*walks to perch*) Hello, Polly-Pat. . . . Hello, Polly-Pat. . . . Hello, Polly-Pat. . . .
POLLY-PAT:	Squawk! Whistle!
CHILD:	No! No! Just listen and say this. Hello, Polly-Pat. . . . Hello, Polly-Pat. . . . Hello, Polly-Pat.
POLLY-PAT:	Squawk! Whistle!
CHILD:	No, no, no! Don't squawk and whistle like that. Listen carefully. Hello, Polly-Pat. . . . Hello, Polly-Pat. . . . Hello, Polly-Pat.

POLLY-PAT: Squawk! Whistle!

CHILD: Oh, dear, she's not catching on to this at all. Well, I'll try again later.

BUSTER: (*enters*) Woof! Woof! (*licks child's face*)

CHILD: Oh, Buster, how's my good old dog? (*pats him with free hand*) You're a smart doggie. How would you like to learn some tricks? There must be several chapters in this book about training dogs. Let me see. (*looks at book*) . . . Ah, yes, here's something. (*reads*) "Rolling Over: When your dog is sitting, push him firmly down onto his side and say, 'Roll over.' At the same time make a big, rolling-over motion with one hand." Okay, here goes. . . . Buster, I'm glad you're sitting down, because I am going to push you over on your side. (*pushes dog*) Lie down, Buster. Good dog! Now, roll over. (*motions*) . . . Roll over. (*motions*) . . . Roll over. (*motions*) . . . Hmmmmm, maybe that's too difficult. I'll try something else. There must be *something* easier in this book. (*looks at book*) . . . Yes, here's an idea. (*reads*) "Teaching Your Dog to Speak on Command: Show your dog a biscuit and say, 'Speak.' When he barks, give him the biscuit and praise him." The cookie I have here in my pocket should work. Buster loves cookies. (*reaches into pocket and thrusts hand toward dog*) Here, Buster, see the nice cookie? Chocolate chip, your favorite. Mmmmm, good! I'll give it to you if you speak. Speak, Buster. . . . Speak. . . . Speak. . . . Speak. . . . Oh, rats! This is harder than I thought it would be. I'll eat the cookie myself. I will try again later, but now I'm going out to play. (*exits*) . . .

POLLY-PAT: Hello, Polly-Pat. . . . Hello, Polly-Pat. . . . Hello, Polly-Pat. Squawk! Whistle! (*dog bounces to parrot perch*) . . . Roll over, Buster. (*dog rolls*) . . . Roll

over. (*dog rolls*) . . . Roll over. (*dog rolls*) . . . Good
dog! Squawk! Whistle!. . . Speak, Buster.

BUSTER: Woof!

POLLY-PAT: Speak.

BUSTER: Woof!

POLLY-PAT: Speak.

BUSTER: Woof! Woof! Woof!

POLLY-PAT: Good doggie! Squawk! Whistle!

Clever Pets

Production notes

PUPPETS:

The child, who may resemble either a girl or a boy, must be a hand-action puppet, because he/she is required to hold a book in one hand and gesticulate with the other. Its apparel should have a patch pocket on the side which has a free hand. Buster should also be a hand-action puppet so that most of the body can be seen by the audience. Polly-Pat should be a silhouette bird, cut out of poster board and painted bright green and yellow. If the head is a separate piece attached to the body with a short length of green pipe cleaner, it will wobble slightly and seem more alive.

SETTING:

The parrot perch, which remains onstage for the entire play, should be placed well to the right to allow room for the action. It should be taped to the frame of the puppet stage. No prop stage is needed.

PROPS:

A short length of dowel with an ice cream stick attached for a crossbar will serve as a perch, and the parrot can be glued to that. The book, which must be attached to the child's hand, should appear to be open for reading. It can be made of cardboard and several folds of paper stapled together.

TAPING:

The sounds made by the dog and parrot should be as realistic as possible. The parrot's raucous squawk should be followed immediately by a piercing double-toned whistle. The person who records the child's part should have a medium-range voice and enunciate clearly, paying careful attention to the pauses.

ACTION: Since the parrot's perch is at the right, the child and dog should enter from the left, and the child should exit left. The puppeteer on the left can play both parts. The child's book should be attached to the arm that fits the puppeteer's thumb. The index finger will fit into the head, allowing the middle finger to be the arm that makes the turning motion. The puppeteer on the right can operate the tape player and jiggle the perch slightly when the parrot squawks, whistles, or talks.

TIME: 5 minutes. Allow extra time for introductory music.

FISHING

CHARACTERS

SALLY
TOMMY
LADY
LITTLE BOY

PROPS

FISHING POLE
POT
PICTURE FRAME
JUNK (3 PIECES)
"GARAGE SALE" SIGN
FISH

SALLY: (*enters singing*)

La-da-de-da-da-da,
La-da-de-da-da-da,
La-da-de-da-da-da,
Bumpity-bump-bump, bump-bump!

I am so bored. I don't have anything to do, anything fun, that is. . . . Of course, when I said that to my Mom, she said I could pick up my toys and clean my messy room. Well, that's not at all what I had in mind. . . . Hmmmmm, what do you know? Here I am at Tommy's house. I wonder if he's home. I'll just knock on his door. (*knocks*)

TOMMY: (*enters*) Hi, Sally. What's new?

SALLY: What's new? Nothing, absolutely nothing. I can't think of anything fun to do. Can you come out to play?

TOMMY: Sorry, not today. I have big plans.

SALLY: What? Tell me, tell me, tell me.

TOMMY: Okay, okay, okay. I'll tell you. Today I am going fishing.

SALLY: Fishing! Oh, frabjous day! May I come along? I'd like to go fishing.

TOMMY: Well, I don't know. I don't think so.

SALLY: But I know I'd love fishing. Please take me along. Please, please, ple-e-eze.

TOMMY: But I have only one fishing pole.

SALLY: That's all right. I'll just watch.

TOMMY: Well, okay. Wait here and I'll go get my pole. (*exits and returns with pole*) . . . All right, let's go. (*crosses stage and exits followed by Sally . . . and they reenter*) . . . Here we are at the pond. This grassy bank looks like a good spot, and don't you think the fish will like this nice juicy worm? (*flips it in Sallys face*)

SALLY: Yuk! Get that away from me. Remember, I'm just watching.

TOMMY: Oh, that's right. Well, now I think I'll drop my nice, juicy worm into the water about here. (*drops line*) Come on, fish, it's time for lunch.

SALLY: Any bites?

TOMMY: No, not yet, silly. Hey, wait a minute. I think I feel something nibbling on my juicy worm.

SALLY: Oh, it must be a big one. Look at your pole bending.

TOMMY: I'll give it a good yank. . . . No, I can't do it.

SALLY: Pull harder.

TOMMY: (*struggling with pole*) I'm pulling as hard as I can.

SALLY: Maybe it's a whale.

TOMMY: Or a whale of a big fish.

SALLY:	Let me help.
TOMMY:	No, you're only watching, remember? Ah, here it comes. (*pulls up pot*)
SALLY:	Ha-ha-ha! That's someone's old cooking pot. Here, let me take it off the hook, and we'll throw it back in the pond.
TOMMY:	No, don't throw it back. I don't want to catch it again. (*Sally removes pot and sets it aside.*) . . .
SALLY:	Go on and try again.
TOMMY:	All right. (*drops line*) Maybe I'll have better luck this time. Ah-oh, I think I have a bite. Stand back while I pull him in. (*pulls up picture frame*)
SALLY:	Nothing but an old picture frame. Well, I'll take it off the hook, and we'll put it here with the cooking pot. (*removes frame and sets it aside*) . . .
TOMMY:	Maybe third time's the charm. Here goes. (*drops line*) Surely there's a fish down there somewhere. Oh, I feel something on my line again. I hope it's a fish this time. Cross your fingers, Sally. (*pulls up a piece of junk*) Phooey! It's not fish, of course. It's a hunk of junk.
SALLY:	I'll take it off and put it here with the other stuff. (*removes junk and sets it aside*) . . .
TOMMY:	I'll try again. (*drops line and pulls up another piece of junk*) . . . More junk! I can't believe it.
SALLY:	I'll take it off. (*removes junk and sets it aside*) . . .
TOMMY:	I'll try one more time. (*drops line and pulls up another piece of junk*) Oh, crumbs!
SALLY:	I'll add it to the pile. (*removes junk and sets it aside*) . . . Our pile is growing bigger.
TOMMY:	I give up. I'm going home.
SALLY:	No! You stay here and guard the junk. I have a great idea. Don't go away. I'll be right back. (*exits*)

TOMMY:	(*calls after her*) Guard the junk? Sally, you've got to be crazy. Who would want this stuff? Well, she said she'd be right back, so I might as well wait. At least it's a nice day. . . . Hey, is that Sally coming back already? Yes, here she comes.
SALLY:	(*enters with sign*) See, I said I'd be right back. Look what I have.
TOMMY:	That sign says, "Garage Sale." Why did you bring it to the pond?
SALLY:	Because we're going to have a sale right here and get rid of all this stuff.
TOMMY:	But there's no garage here.
SALLY:	That doesn't matter. I'll stick this sign up near the road and we'll wait for business. (*exits with sign*)
TOMMY:	Sally sure is a crazy girl. No one is going to buy this junk.
SALLY:	(*enters*) This is going to be great. I see a customer coming already.
LADY:	(*enters*) Oh, what a beautiful cooking pot! How much is it?
TOMMY:	Uh-uh-uh, I don't know.
SALLY:	It's fifty cents.
LADY:	Very well, here's your money. (*show of money exchange*)
SALLY:	Thank you very much. Good-bye, and have a nice day. (*Lady exits with pot*) . . .
LADY:	(*enters*) I remembered this lovely picture frame. How much is it?
SALLY:	That's fifty cents, too.
LADY:	What a bargain! Well, here's your money. (*show of money exchange*)
SALLY:	Thanks again. Good-bye, and have a nice day. (*Lady exits with picture frame*) . . .

LADY:	(*enters*) I can't help myself. I just can't resist garage sales. I'll buy everything you have left, if you give me a good price.
SALLY:	All right, a dollar for everything!
LADY:	Wonderful! Would you help me put it in my car?
SALLY:	Yes, ma'am! (*they exit with remaining junk, Sally making two trips*)
TOMMY:	Sally was right. A garage sale was a good idea. This pond is filled with everything except fish. . . .
SALLY:	(*enters*) Tommy, we sold all of the junk, and I have the two dollars in my pocket. This hasn't been a boring day after all. And we have enough money to go to the Dairy Bar for ice cream cones.
TOMMY:	Great idea! But, look, someone else is coming.
LITTLE BOY:	(*enters*) Am I too late for the garage sale?
SALLY:	Yes. I'm sorry, but we've sold everything, and we're leaving.
LITTLE BOY:	What about the fishing pole? I'd really like to fish in this nice pond.
TOMMY:	You poor kid! This pond is full of junk, not fish. So take my pole as a gift.
LITTLE BOY:	For free? Oh, thank you very much.
TOMMY:	You're welcome. Come on, Sally. Let's go off to the Dairy Bar. (*exits with Sally*)
LITTLE BOY:	I really like this fishing pole, and a nice juicy worm is still on the hook. I'll throw it in. Maybe I'll catch some junk, too. (*drops line*) . . . Wait, I'm caught on something. . . . Here it comes! (*pulls in fish and exits laughing*)

Fishing

Production notes

PUPPETS: All of the characters should be hand-action puppets so that they can maneuver the props.

SETTING: A prop stage is necessary, and, if temporary, it must be large enough to hold all of the junk and be placed at left of center. The change of scene from just outside Tommy's house to the pond is accomplished by the exit and reentrance of the two main characters. If a temporary prop stage is used, it should be in place from the beginning of the play. Even though it's not needed until later, it would be more distracting to put it up in the middle of the action than to have it there from the start.

PROPS: The fishing pole can be a stick with several inches of line securely attached. The hook (not a barbed one) can be made from a paper clip with a rubber band for a worm. Any small pot will do, but it must have a handle or some means of fitting easily on the hook. The picture frame can be made of cardboard or ice cream sticks. The three remaining pieces of junk are purposely not described so that whatever is available can be used, such as the wheel of a toy truck, a piece of doll furniture, a measuring spoon, etc.—any small item that the hook can hold. The garage sale sign can be made of poster board glued to an ice cream stick and the fish made of painted cardboard. All of the props must have a handle, hole, or loop that will fit on the hook (excepting the sign).

TAPING: The sound of knocking on the door is the only sound effect needed. Sally and Tommy should have children's voices, but they should sound different because they converse. The lady should speak like a stock company matron and the little boy like a very young child. Pauses and directions must be carefully observed to allow sufficient time for the necessary stage business.

ACTION: The puppeteer on the left should be Sally and the lady. The puppeteer on the right should be Tommy and the little boy and can operate the tape player. Sally enters from the left, crosses the stage, and knocks on Tommy's imaginary door at the right. Tommy first enters, exits, and reenters from the right (his house). Then both characters cross stage, exit left, and reenter to establish the change of scene. Subsequent entrances and exits by all characters should be made on the left side. The fishing line is dropped out of sight to the rear so that the puppeteer on the right can slip the props onto the hook. When the lady gives money to Sally, it is an imaginary exchange.

TIME: 9 minutes. Allow extra time for introductory music.

COUCH POTATOES

CHARACTERS
  NARRATOR
  SPUD
  TATER
  MISSY MUSCLE (NOT SEEN)*

PROPS
  COUCH
  REMOTE CONTROL

NARRATOR: Oh, what a beautiful morning! Children everywhere are bounding out of bed. They can hardly wait to go outside to play . . . or, perhaps I am mistaken. Here come two who are certainly not bounding. This is Spud . . . (*Spud enters slowly*) . . . and this is his sister Tater. . . . (*Tater enters even more slowly*) . . . No one can say these kids are bouncing.

SPUD: Oh, man, am I tired!

TATER: Me, too, and I don't know why. I just got up after sleeping ten hours.

SPUD: Thank goodness the couch is right here. (*collapses onto couch*)

TATER: (*sits down beside Spud*) You said it! Ah, it feels good to sit down.

NARRATOR: How pitiful! Those two lazy kids could hardly creep as far as the couch. Just look at them stretching and yawning. (*Spud and Tater stretch*) Are they going to sit there all day doing nothing?

SPUD: I wonder what's on television.

*Missy Muscle appears to lead exercises in the audience participation piece, "Exercise Time."

TATER: You're sitting on the remote control. If you can move just a bit, I'll turn on the TV set.

SPUD: I'll try. (*shifts slightly*) There, can you reach it now?

TATER: Yes, Here goes. (*set clicks on*)

SPUD: Rats! A boring old movie.

TATER: Yes, it is, and we should know. We've seen it four or five times already. I'll try another channel. (*set clicks*) . . .

SPUD: Bleah! Another old movie, and not a good one either, if I remember correctly.

TATER: You're so right, and we've seen this one six or seven times. I'll try again. (*set clicks*) . . .

SPUD: Now it's nothing but snow. Turn on some cartoons.

TATER: I'm trying. I'm trying. (*click . . . click . . . click*) . . . It's no use. There's nothing on.

SPUD: Did you try Channel 13?

TATER: Oh, I forgot. Well, here goes. It's our last chance. (*click*) . . .

NARRATOR: Ah, at last something different is coming on. It's not a cartoon program. It's not an old movie either, and it's not snow. It's . . . "The Missy Muscle Show!" Spud and Tater are settling back to watch. Tater turns up the volume. Let's listen. . . .

MISSY MUSCLE: All right! It's time to exercise. We'll start with some kicks. . . . One . . . two . . . one . . . two . . . one . . . two . . . Hey, you out there! Get off that couch.

SPUD: Does she mean us?

TATER: Are you crazy? Of course she doesn't mean us. People on TV can't see us.

MISSY MUSCLE: Hah! That's what you think. I can see you all right. I can see that you are frazzled and sluggish,

	because all you do is sit on that stupid couch and watch any old garbage that happens to be on this television set. In fact, you two kids are nothing but "Couch Potatoes."
SPUD:	We are not.
TATER:	How dare you call us "Couch Potatoes"?
MISSY MUSCLE:	Because that's the right name for lazy lumps like you. Now, you two, stand up. . . . I'm waiting. . . . Stand up. . . . (*Spud and Tater stand*) Fine! I'm delighted that you can stand. It's a start. Now, it's exercise time. Watch and do everything exactly as I do. (*Spud and Tater follow directions*) Bend to the right, like this. . . . Bend to the left, like this. . . . Bend to the right. . . . Bend to the left. . . . Bend to the right. . . . Bend to the left. . . . Bend right. . . . Bend left. . . . Jump! Jump! Jump! . . . Excellent!
SPUD:	Are we done? Can we stop now?
TATER:	I'm tired. I want to take a break.
MISSY MUSCLE:	No way. We're just getting started. Don't you dare sit down. Here we go again. . . . Twist right like this. . . . Twist left like this. . . . Twist right. . . . . . .Twist left. . . . Twist right. . . . Twist left. . . . Touch your toes. . . . Stand up. . . . Touch your toes. . . . Stand up. . . . Touch your toes. . . . Stand up. . . . Jump! Jump! Jump!. . . Wonderful! Now it's time to jog in place. You two start. I'll keep the rhythm going. . . . Jog, jog, Couch Potatoes, jog. Jog, jog, Couch Potatoes, jog. . . . Jog, jog, Couch Potatoes, jog. . . . Jog, jog, Couch Potatoes, jog. . . . Jog, jog, jog, jog, jog, jog, jog. . . . Now run out the door, around the block, and back again. Jog, jog, jog, jog, jog, jog, jog. (*Spud and Tater exit*)
NARRATOR:	Well, there they go. Missy Muscle really got Spud and Tater to move. . . . They're turning the first

corner. . . . Now they're rounding the second. . . . They're picking up speed. They're going faster, faster. . . . It's amazing! They're almost 'round the block. Here they come now. (*Spud and Tater enter*)

MISSY MUSCLE: Say, kids, that was very good. I really didn't think you could do it. You seem so full of life now, not at all like lumpy-bumpy-dumpy potatoes. And guess what! You actually look slimmer!

SPUD: She's right, Tater. I do feel livelier.

TATER: Me, too! I feel so much better. And we *are* slimmer, so we not only feel better, but we look better, too.

SPUD: I have a good idea. It's such a nice day. Let's play outside.

TATER: Yes, let's. But first I'd better turn off the TV. (*goes to couch and touches remote control*) Good-bye, Missy Muscle, and thanks. (*set clicks off*) Well, let's go. (*Spud and Tater exit jogging*)

NARRATOR: So at last Spud and Tater are outside enjoying the beautiful morning. We can't call them "Couch Potatoes" anymore.

Couch Potatoes

Production notes

PUPPETS:

Spud and Tater should not look like real children, but the simplest type of hand-action puppets. Each should consist of two flat pieces of light brown fabric cut to fit the puppeteer's hand with projections for thumb and two fingers. Eyes and mouth can be tiny circles of black felt glued to the face area. Tater should have a pink bow attached on top to indicate that she is female. At first they should look lumpily round like real potatoes, so some padding in front is needed. This could be secured with Velcro and removed during their jogging. Since the puppets are so simple to make, another option would be to have two sets of puppets, "before" and "after." If this is done, the round mouths could be replaced by smiling ones.

SETTING:

To create the living room setting the only thing needed is the couch, which remains for the duration of the play since the scene doesn't change. It must be secured to a permanent (or temporary) prop stage or possibly to the puppet stage frame itself. It should be sufficiently off center to the left to allow the puppets room to exercise. Since Spud and Tater face front, the television set is left to the audience's imagination.

PROPS:

Since Spud and Tater are a plain light brown, the couch should be a contrasting color or pattern. A flattened roll of fabric or an elongated bean bag could be used. It should not have a back, because the puppets, held from behind, must seem to be sitting on top. The remote control could be any tiny rectangular shape glued to the top.

TAPING: Spud and Tater are both children, so their voices should be high but noticeably different in pitch and tone since they converse. They should speak slowly, befitting their sluggish condition, until they return from jogging. Missy Muscle should have a bossy female voice. The narrator may be any good reader, but a man's voice would provide a good contrast. The TV remote clicks, which are the only sound effect, should be loud, and timing is important.

ACTION: The puppeteer on the right should operate the tape player and the one on the left should be both Spud and Tater. This best enables the puppets' exercises to be coordinated. They should enter first from the left and make all other exits and entrances from the right. The narrator and Missy Muscle describe much of the action, and it may help to know that in conversation Spud always speaks first. This play can be produced with a minimum of rehearsal.

TIME: 7 minutes. Allow extra time for introductory music.

LITTERBUGS

CHARACTERS*

BRYAN
SUSIE
FLYSWATTER

PROPS

CANDY WRAPPER
NOTE
2 BAGS OF TRASH
TRASH CAN

BRYAN:
(*enters, eating candy bar*) Yum, yum, yum. What a delicious candy bar! . . . (*eats*) . . . Mmmmm, absolutely yummy! . . . Oh, my, it's all gone. Nothing left but this dumb old candy wrapper. Now, what should I do with the candy wrapper? . . . Let me consider this. . . . I could put it in my pocket, I guess, . . . but, no. Why should I mess up my pocket with trash? . . . I know what I'll do. I'll just throw it down on the sidewalk. . . . (*throws down wrapper*) There! (*exits*)

SUSIE:
(*enters holding note*) I wish I didn't have to go home today. I wish I didn't have a mean old teacher, and Ms. Watch-yer-step *is* a mean old teacher. You better believe it! She is mean, mean, mean. She's always telling me that I talk too much. She says that when I talk in school I disturb the other children. The nerve of her! She says I talk all the time about anything and everything, and sometimes *nothing*. She wants me to work, work, work. How boring! . . . Instead of working she says I talk, talk, talk. . . . How interesting! . . . And now mean old Ms. Watch-yer-step is sending this note

*Bryan and Susie are also in the audience participation piece, "Throw It in the Litter Bin."

133

	home to my mother. Oh, dear. I am so miserable. (*cries*)
BRYAN:	(*enters*) Hi, Susie.
SUSIE:	(*mournfully*) Hi, Bryan.
BRYAN:	What's the matter, Susie? You sound sad, not at all like your usual super-happy self.
SUSIE:	You're right about that. I *am* sad. My mean old teacher, Ms. Watch-yer-step, sent this note home to my mother, and I'm going to be in trouble.
BRYAN:	That's too bad. What does the note say?
SUSIE:	I don't know exactly, but I sure can guess.
BRYAN:	Well, let's read it and find out.
SUSIE:	Oh, I don't think we should.
BRYAN:	Why not?
SUSIE:	Because the note is addressed to my mother.
BRYAN:	But it's about *you*.
SUSIE:	Y-e-s. You're right about that. . . . Okay, let's read it. (*read imitating teacher's voice*) It says: . . . "Dear Mrs. Strubblemeyer, your daughter Susan is constantly disrupting my class, because, to be brutally frank, she talks too much. Please explain to her that this is very, very rude". . . . And it's signed, "Sincerely yours, Ermintrude Watch-yer-step". . . . See, I told you. I'm going to be in trouble, deep, deep trouble.
BRYAN:	Maybe not. I have an idea.
SUSIE:	Oh, goody! Any idea that could keep me out of trouble would be fine.
BRYAN:	Okay, then. You just throw that note away. Ms. Watch-yer-step will never know. After all, she didn't ask your mother to write back.

SUSIE:	You're right, Bryan, and that's a great idea. I *will* throw the note away. (*flings note aside*) Good-bye-e-e, mean old note from mean old Ms. Watch-yer-step. . . . (*dances and claps hands*) I feel so much better. Now my troubles are over.
FLYSWATTER:	(*enters from above*) Oh, no, they're not. Your troubles are not over. Your troubles are just beginning.
BRYAN/SUSIE:	(*cowering*) Help! Help! Help!
FLYSWATTER:	(*laughs meanly*) You'd better cry for help, you miserable creatures.
SUSIE:	What is that big thing? . . . Who-who-who *are* you?
FLYSWATTER:	(*in booming voice*) I am the Giant Flyswatter in the Sky, and *I* am going to get you.
BRYAN:	But a flyswatter is for bugs. We're not bugs. We're kids.
FLYSWATTER:	Oh, I can see that you are kids. What do you think I am, a dummy? But you are also the worst kind of insects, because you are *litterbugs*!
SUSIE:	Litterbugs? What do you mean?
FLYSWATTER:	What do I mean? Silly girl! I mean that you are throwing your nasty trash all over the place. You are making a mess of this beautiful neighborhood. You are making a mess of the *world*.
BRYAN:	But we threw away only a few bits of paper. You can't punish us for that.
FLYSWATTER:	Oh, yes I can. Just you watch me. (*laughs and flails as Bryan and Susie dodge*)
BRYAN/SUSIE:	Help! Help! Help!
FLYSWATTER:	(*stops flailing*) Do you give up?
BRYAN/SUSIE:	No! No! No!
FLYSWATTER:	Then I'll get you good! (*flails*)

BRYAN/SUSIE: Help! Help! We give up! We give up!

FLYSWATTER: (*pausing*) Are you sure?

BRYAN/SUSIE: Yes! Yes! Yes! We're sure. We're sure.

FLYSWATTER: Very well, then. I'll stop my swatting for a while, but I'm still not positive that you've learned your lesson.

BRYAN: What do we have to do to prove we've learned our lesson? Please tell us. We'll do anything you say if you'll leave us alone.

FLYSWATTER: Well, let me think. . . . Aha! Yes, I know exactly what you should do.

SUSIE: What? What should we do?

FLYSWATTER: Believing that the punishment should fit the crime, *I*, the Giant Flyswatter in the Sky, hereby pronounce your sentence. You two miserable litterbugs must go forth and pick up every bit of litter in this neighborhood. That means every can, every ice cream stick, and every scrap of paper, including little, tiny, teensy-weensy pieces. And you might as well start with the candy wrapper and that note from Ms. Watch-yer-step. When you're finished, bring all of that trash right back to me. I'll be waiting, so you'd better be quick about it.

BRYAN: All right. All right. We'll hurry. We'll be back soon. (*Bryan and Susie exit*)

FLYSWATTER: Well, there go a couple of dummies. But maybe, just maybe, I scared them a little. I'll have to wait and see. . . . Ah, yes, from my fine position up here in the sky, I can easily observe what's happening down below. (*laughs happily*) They really are working, and very fast, too, I might add. My goodness, I believe they're coming back. They took me at my word and were quick about it.

BRYAN:	(*enters with bag of trash*) We did it as fast as we could. We picked up every piece of litter that we found.
SUSIE:	(*enters with bag of trash*) Bryan's right. We picked up every teensy-weensy bit we saw.
FLYSWATTER:	Yes, I believe you did, and I hate to admit it, but I'm proud of you.
BRYAN:	Now, may we go home?
SUSIE:	Please, please, may we? My mother will be worried.
FLYSWATTER:	Yes, you may leave, but first deposit those bags of trash in my giant trash can.
SUSIE:	All right, but where is it?
FLYSWATTER:	Right here. Kazoom! (*swats and trash can rises into view*) . . . Now, toss in those bags of litter while I'm still in a good mood.
SUSIE:	Okay, here's mine. (*puts bag into can*)
BRYAN:	And here's mine, too. (*puts bag into can*) Now may we go home? (*trash can sinks from sight*)
SUSIE:	Please, please, please. My mother will be very, very, *very* worried.
FLYSWATTER:	Well, I don't want her to worry. Off you go! But, remember, you have to promise me, *no more littering*.
SUSIE:	No more littering. I promise. (*exits*)
BRYAN:	I promise, too. No more littering. (*exits*)
FLYSWATTER:	I do believe that those two have learned their lesson, and I notice that Susie has found that note she threw away. She's putting it in her pocket, so I guess she's going to give it to her mother after

all. . . . But what do I see down the street?
Someone is throwing a hamburger box in the
gutter. Hey! Hey, you, down there! You're a
litterbug, and *I* am going to get you! (*exits
swatting*)

Litterbugs

PUPPETS:
Bryan and Susie must be hand-action puppets capable of holding the candy wrapper and note and manipulating the bags of trash. The Flyswatter, a combination character/prop, should not be so long in the handle that its movement will interfere with the other action. To preserve the proper illusion, the hand holding the Flyswatter should be covered, preferably by a heavy-duty white workman's glove.

SETTING:
No prop stage is needed. The litter dropped onto the street by the puppets can fall onto the floor backstage, and a puppeteer can hold the trash can, which is needed only briefly.

PROPS:
The candy wrapper can be from any candy bar. It should be partially folded so that it may seem to be eaten before being tossed away. The note may be a small scribbled piece of memo paper. The trash bags should be transparent plastic, filled with wads of paper and not too large or heavy for the puppets to manage. The trash can may be any food can tall and wide enough to hold the filled bags.

TAPING:
No sound effects are needed. Bryan's should be a little boy's voice. He should speak slowly. Susie's pitch should be somewhat higher, and she should speak faster. The Flyswatter should have a booming male voice and speak with authority.

139

ACTION: The puppeteer on the left should be both Bryan and Susie. Except for Susie's first entrance from the right, these puppets should always enter and exit from the left. The puppeteer on the right should operate the tape player and take the part of the Flyswatter. The Flyswatter enters from top right and remains there. This leaves a free hand for the puppeteer to produce the trash can. This can need be raised only enough so that it's visible to the audience. It can slowly sink from sight when it is no longer needed.

TIME: 9 $^1/_2$ minutes. Allow extra time for introductory music.

LOST IN A FAIRY TALE

CHARACTERS

NARRATOR
GOLDILOCKS
LITTLE RED RIDING HOOD
HANSEL
GRETEL
FROG
GINGERBREAD BOY
PIG
FAIRY GODMOTHER

PROPS

BASKET
PIECE OF
  GINGERBREAD
BAG
WAND

NARRATOR:	Once upon a time there was a little girl named Goldilocks. . . . Oh, I know what you're thinking. You think you're going to hear about her adventure with the Three Bears. But you're wrong. This adventure starts where the old one left off. Goldilocks has just escaped from the house of the Three Bears. Here she comes now racing through the woods, lickety-split.
GOLDILOCKS:	(*enters puffing and panting*) . . . Help! . . . Help! . . .
NARRATOR:	What's the matter, Goldilocks?
GOLDILOCKS:	Three grouchy bears are about to get me.
NARRATOR:	There's no one chasing you, Goldilocks.
GOLDILOCKS:	(*looks*) Oh! By gummy, you're right. Well, that was a lucky escape. Now I guess I'd better go home.
NARRATOR:	That sounds like a splendid idea. Do you know where home is?

GOLDILOCKS: Oh, sure. It's this way. (*points*) Or maybe it's that way. (*points*) . . . Oh, no! I don't know which way to go. I'm lost. (*whimpers*)

NARRATOR: Goldilocks, you might as well dry your eyes. Crying won't help.

GOLDILOCKS: (*wails*) But what am I going to do?

NARRATOR: Well, since you asked, I suggest you stop running and start walking. Perhaps you will meet someone who will give you directions.

GOLDILOCKS: I hope you're right. I do want to get home.

NARRATOR: Then I think you should continue slowly down this path and see what happens.

GOLDILOCKS: I might as well. I have to find my way home somehow. (*starts off*) Oh, dear me, the path forks here. . . . Which way should I go? The fork to the right goes uphill. The fork to the left goes downhill. . . . I am so tired from all that running that I think downhill is best. (*walks*) . . . Someone's coming. Why, it's a little girl just like me.

LITTLE RED: (*enters holding basket*) Hello. Who are you, and what are you doing here in the woods?

GOLDILOCKS: My name is Goldilocks, and I'm lost. Who are you?

LITTLE RED: I'm called Little Red Riding Hood. I'll bet you can guess why.

GOLDILOCKS: I imagine it's because of that gorgeous red cloak and hood you're wearing.

LITTLE RED: Right you are. This outfit was a gift from my dear granny. But you still haven't told me why you're wandering lost in the woods.

GOLDILOCKS: Well, it's quite a story. I was taking a walk in the woods near my house when I came upon a pretty little cottage. No one was home at the time, so I went inside to have a look around. It wasn't till later that I learned that the place belongs to a family of bears. I just happened to be taking a little nap in one of their beds when in they came, Mama, Papa, and Baby! And were they ever mad! Well, maybe I shouldn't have eaten their porridge or sat in their chairs or lain in their beds, but that was no reason for them to get so huffy. What a bunch of grumps!

LITTLE RED: With good reason, I'd say.

GOLDILOCKS: Anyway, I decided I'd better get out of there, and fast! I hope I don't meet any other bears.

LITTLE RED: It isn't bears you have to watch out for here. It's wolves. What just happened to me is much, much worse than your adventure with the bears. I was delivering a basket of goodies to my poor, sick granny who lives not far from here, and when I got to her house I found that a wicked wolf had swallowed her whole. And, guess what! Then he had me for dessert.

GOLDILOCKS: How awful! How ever did you manage to escape after being eaten?

LITTLE RED: A huntsman happened by, lucky for me. If he hadn't slit that old wolf open, I wouldn't be talking to you now.

GOLDILOCKS: (*wails*) Oh, now I'm more frightened than ever. First bears and now wolves! I'm afraid I'll never get home.

LITTLE RED: Don't worry. You'll be all right as long as you stick to the path. . . . Well, I'm sorry, but I have to leave you now. I hope you find your way home all right, Goldilocks. (*exits*)

GOLDILOCKS: So do I. So do I. . . . Somehow I feel I'm headed the wrong way. I think perhaps I should go back and take the other fork in the path. (*turns back briefly and continues*) Here it is. I sure hope this is the right direction out of this scary place. . . . Do I see

someone coming this way? . . .Yes, it's a boy and
a girl. Maybe they can help me. (*Hansel and Gretel
enter, Hansel holding gingerbread*)

HANSEL: Hello, little girl.

GOLDILOCKS: Hello to you. My name is Goldilocks, and I'm lost.
                 Can you tell me how to get out of the woods?

HANSEL: We're lost, too. My name is Hansel, and this is my
                 sister Gretel.

GRETEL: We have just escaped from a wicked witch who
                 was planning to eat us.

GOLDILOCKS: Why, that's terrible. I've just had a lucky escape,
                 too. The Three Bears were a bit grouchy, but I
                 don't think they were planning to eat me. . . . Did
                 you say that you are lost, too? You don't seem a bit
                 worried about getting home.

HANSEL: We know we'll find our way sooner or later, and
                 meanwhile we have plenty to eat. . . . Would you
                 like some gingerbread or candy? (*offers it*)

GRETEL: The witch's house was made of gingerbread and
                 other luscious things, and we took some when we
                 left.

GOLDILOCKS: Usually I wouldn't say no to gingerbread or candy,
                 but not long ago I polished off a bowl of porridge.
                 Now all I want is to get home.

HANSEL: Do you want to come with us? We're going this
                 way. (*points*)

GOLDILOCKS: No, thanks. I've just come from there. I think I'd
                 better continue the way I'm headed now.

H. & G.:   Then good-bye, Goldilocks. (*exit*)

GOLDILOCKS: Good-bye. (*moves in opposite direction*) Maybe I
                 should have gone with Hansel and Gretel. I'd
                 better stop for a while and think.

FROG: (*from offstage*) Rib-bit. . . . Rib-bit. . . .

GOLDILOCKS:	That sounds like a frog.
FROG:	(*enters hopping*) Right you are. I'm a frog, but in body only.
GOLDILOCKS:	I've never heard anything so silly. A frog is just a frog, and that's that.
FROG:	You are mistaken. A horrid witch cast a spell on me. I was once a handsome prince, and so shall I be again, but first I must find a beautiful princess to break the spell. Are you, perchance, a princess?
GOLDILOCKS:	I'm afraid not. I'm just a poor little girl lost in these frightful woods. I know nothing about breaking spells.
FROG:	Then, alas, you cannot help me, and I fear I cannot help you either. So, I must leave you. Good-bye, Goldilocks, I truly hope you find your way home. (*exits*)
GOLDILOCKS:	(*calls after him*) Good-bye, Your Highness, I hope you find your princess. . . . (*wails*) And I hope *I* find my way home soon. . . . My, goodness, who's that coming in such a rush?
GING. BOY:	(*enters*) I'm the Gingerbread Boy, I am! I am! I've run away from a little old woman and a little old man and a cow and a horse and a barn full of threshers and a field full of mowers, and I can run away from you, I can, I can!
GOLDILOCKS:	Don't be such a dummy. I'm not going to chase you.
GING. BOY:	What? Do you mean you don't want to eat me?
GOLDILOCKS:	No, I'm not at all interested in eating you.
GING. BOY:	I'm certainly glad to hear that. . . . Oh, here they all come chasing me again. I must backtrack and twist to the left. That will fool them, for sure. (*exits the way he entered*)

GOLDILOCKS:	Silly old cookie! He'll end up in *somebody's* tummy, and that's a fact. . . . And I'm beginning to think I'll end up here, lost in these woods forever. (*cries*)
PIG:	(*enters holding bag*) What's the matter, little girl? Why are you crying so?
GOLDILOCKS:	(*sobbing*) Because . . . I'm afraid . . . I'm never going to find my way out of the woods and home.
PIG:	Tell me who you are, little girl, and where you live. Maybe I can help.
GOLDILOCKS:	I am Goldilocks, and if I knew where I lived, I wouldn't be crying. But who are you, or should I say *what* are you?
PIG:	"Who" sounds much more polite. I am the Third Little Pig, the third and last.
GOLDILOCKS:	Whatever do you mean?
PIG:	Perhaps you've heard the sad story called *The Three Little Pigs*.
GOLDILOCKS:	Yes, that sounds familiar. Wasn't there a big, bad wolf in that story?
PIG:	Indeed, yes, but I outwitted him in the end. I am the one who had the sense to build a house of bricks.
GOLDILOCKS:	Now I remember. That old wolf huffed and puffed, but he couldn't blow your house down. So he never got to eat you up.
PIG:	And he couldn't trick me into letting him in either. The old rascal tried, but I said, "No, not by the hair of my chinny chin chin."
GOLDILOCKS:	You don't happen to know Little Red Riding Hood, do you?
PIG:	Can't say I've had the pleasure.
GOLDILOCKS:	It must have been a different wolf. . . . But never

	mind about that. How do *you* happen to be in the woods, and how can you help me?
PIG:	(*shakes bag*) I was gathering acorns. I dearly love acorns. Would you like one? (*offers bag*)
GOLDILOCKS:	No, thanks. What I'd *like* is for you to explain how you can help me. I need all the help I can get.
PIG:	Well, I can't take you to your own front door, but I can, at least, lead you out of the woods.
GOLDILOCKS:	Thank you, Mr. Pig. That would be wonderful.
PIG:	All right, then. Follow me, and we'll be out of here in no time. (*exits*)
GOLDILOCKS:	I'm coming. (*exits*)
PIG:	(*enters followed by Goldilocks*) See, I told you so. A few simple turns, and here we are in the country-side.
GOLDILOCKS:	What a relief! Seeing nothing but dark, gloomy trees was beginning to depress me.
PIG:	I'm glad I could help, Goldilocks. Now, I still have to fill my bag with acorns, so I'll say good-bye to you. (*exits*)
GOLDILOCKS:	(*calls after him*) Good-bye, Mr. Pig, and thanks again. . . .I'm glad to be out of the woods at last, but I still have no idea where home is. I am so miserable. (*sobs*)
FAIRY G.M.:	(*enters holding wand*) My poor child, why are you weeping so?
GOLDILOCKS:	I wish . . . oh, I wish . . .
FAIRY G.M.:	You wish you could find your way home.
GOLDILOCKS:	Why, yes! How did you know, pretty lady?
FAIRY G.M.:	Because I am your Fairy Godmother.
GOLDILOCKS:	I didn't know I had a Fairy Godmother.

FAIRY G.M.:	You never needed one before today. I've just finished a big job, and now I'm ready to help you.
GOLDILOCKS:	Can you really help me?
FAIRY G.M.:	I don't carry around this magic wand for nothing. You should just ask Cinderella what I can do.
GOLDILOCKS:	Cinderella? Are you her Fairy Godmother, too?
FAIRY G.M.:	I was until last Saturday, but now she's married to her handsome prince and lives in a palace. No more mean stepmother or ugly stepsisters, and no more messing about in the cinders. Cinderella doesn't need me anymore.
GOLDILOCKS:	But I do.
FAIRY G.M.:	Yes, my dear.
GOLDILOCKS:	Then, please, please, show me the way home. Is it nearby?
FAIRY G.M.:	No, I'm afraid your home is on the other side of the woods. But don't worry, I will get you there.
GOLDILOCKS:	Oh, goody! How?
FAIRY G.M.:	(*waves wand*) By using this.
GOLDILOCKS:	Your magic wand?
FAIRY G.M.:	Yes, my child. But you must do exactly as I tell you.
GOLDILOCKS:	Oh, I will. I promise.
FAIRY G.M.:	Then listen carefully. You must bow your head and cover your eyes with your hands.
GOLDILOCKS:	(*follows directions*) Like this?
FAIRY G.M.:	That's right. Now, stand very still. I will count slowly to three, and then you may open your eyes. Are you ready?
GOLDILOCKS:	Yes, Fairy Godmother.
FAIRY G.M.:	Then . . . (*waves wand*) One . . . two . . . three! (*exits*)

GOLDILOCKS: (*looks around*) Oh, she's gone! But . . . but . . . I see my house. I'm home, home at last! (*exits*)

NARRATOR: And there goes Goldilocks . . . through the garden gate, . . . over the path . . . and into her house. . . . I'm sure you'll agree that she's had enough excitement for one day. . . . And now you know what happened *after* her adventure with the Three Bears.

Lost in a Fairy Tale

Production notes

PUPPETS: With the exception of the frog, all of the puppets
            should be hand-action, and they should conform
            to a child's perception of the familiar fairy-tale
            characters. Goldilocks should have yellow hair,
            Red Riding Hood a red hooded cape, Gretel an
            apron, and the fairy godmother fancy attire. The
            Gingerbread Boy can be two pieces of tan felt
            sewn together and outlined in white braid. The
            pig can have an ordinary foam ball head with pink
            paper ears and a cylindrical snout cut from a pink
            eraser. The frog, which needs only a head showing,
            should be a green mouth-action puppet with
            appropriately large eyes.

SETTING: The woods, and later the countryside, is entirely
            imaginary, and no prop stage is needed.

PROPS: Red Riding Hood should carry a basket. In lieu of
            a real basket, one could be fashioned of brown
            paper. Hansel's piece of gingerbread can be made
            of corrugated cardboard. The pig's bag can be
            made of any kind of cloth available. The Fairy
            Godmother's wand should have some glitter or
            tinsel on the tip. Since the puppets need carry only
            the props, these may be fastened to the puppets'
            hands, perhaps just one hand, rather than clutched
            in both.

TAPING: No special sound effects are needed. Goldilocks
            should have a distinctive voice, perhaps slightly
            scratchy, that will contrast effectively with the

voices of the other little girl characters. Hansel
and the Gingerbread Boy's voices should be somewhat lower, and the frog's deepest of all. The Fairy
Godmother's voice should be soft and soothing.
The narrator can be any good reader.

ACTION:

The puppeteer on the left should be Goldilocks,
and the puppeteer on the right all of the other
characters. Goldilocks first enters from the left.
All of the other characters enter from the right.
Little Red Riding Hood, Hansel and Gretel, and
the frog all pass Goldilocks on the path, so they
exit left. The Gingerbread Boy changes course, so
he turns and exits right. Goldilocks follows the
pig for the brief exit and reentrance right, and
then the pig passes her and finally exits left. The
Fairy Godmother enters and exits from below, as
if by magic. Then Goldilocks's final exit is to the
left. Either puppeteer can easily manage the tape
player.

TIME:

14 minutes. Allow extra time for introductory
music.

RYAN'S HAT

CHARACTERS

RYAN
MOM
DOG
AMANDA

PROPS

SIGN
HATS (RYAN'S,
    BASEBALL,
    FIRE FIGHTER'S,
    COWBOY,
    PIRATE'S, SANTA'S)

RYAN:	(*enters and starts across stage*)
MOM:	(*calls from offstage*) Ryan. . . Ryan. . .
RYAN:	(*turns*) What? . . . What? . . .
MOM:	(*enters shaking hat*) Ryan, you come back here this minute.
RYAN:	But, Mom, I want to play outside.
MOM:	That's all right, but first come and get your hat.
RYAN:	My hat? Why? I don't want to wear that stupid hat.
MOM:	You don't want to get the sniffles either, do you?
RYAN:	I won't get the sniffles. It's not at all cold outside today, and the sun is shining.
MOM:	You have just gotten over a nasty cold. You are not to leave this house without a hat on your head.
RYAN:	But, Mom. . . .
MOM:	Don't argue, young man. No hat, no playing outside. (*exits*)

152

RYAN: Stupid old hat! Well, I guess I'd better go put it on. (*exits and reenters wearing hat . . . addresses audience*) I told you it was stupid. Well, never mind. I won't be wearing it for long. Heh-heh-heh-heh.

MOM: (*enters and calls*) Ryan. . . Ryan. . .

RYAN: (*turns*) What? . . . What? . . .

MOM: Promise me that you won't take off that hat while you're playing.

RYAN: (*addresses audience*) Maybe it's true what they say. Maybe moms really can read their kids' minds.

MOM: Ryan, I'm waiting. Promise me that you won't take your hat off.

RYAN: All right. All right. I promise.

MOM: Very well. You may run off and play then. (*exits*)

RYAN: Now what will I do? If my friends see me wearing a hat today, they'll laugh at me. But I *did* promise my mother that I wouldn't take it off. . . . Oh! I just thought of something. Maybe the wind will blow it off. That would be the perfect way to get rid of it. (*sighs*) But, no, that's not going to happen. There's not enough wind today. . . But I have another idea. Mom said that I shouldn't *take* it off. She didn't say not to *shake* it off. So that's what I'll do. (*leans over and shakes*) Gee, this is harder than I thought. I'll try again. (*leans and shakes hat off*) There! Well, how about that? My hat fell off. No mother could blame a child if something *falls* off. But I'm sure if Mom knew that my hat *fell* off she'd want me to pick it up. So that's what I'll do. And then—heh-heh-heh—instead of putting it back on my head, I'll put it over here under this bush. (*deposits hat side stage*) Later I'll get it and wear it home. . . . And now I'm off to play. . . . Oh, I see my good friends down the street. (*shouts*) Hey, Vinnie and Joey, are you guys

	going to the park? . . . Okay, wait up. I'll go with you. (*exits*) . . .
DOG:	(*enters*) Woof! Woof! (*sniffs about the stage stopping at hat*) Mmmmmm. Woof! (*picks up hat and exits*) . . .
RYAN:	(*enters*) Worse luck! Here I am back already, and it's all Mom's fault for making me wear that stupid hat. If she hadn't made me do that, I bet I wouldn't have forgotten my Frisbee™. And that reminds me, I'd better put the hat on before I go into my house, just in case Mom sees me. (*searches for hat*) Where is it? I know I left it right here under this bush. . . . (*wails*) Oh, oh, ooooh! It's gone. What am I going to do? I'll be in big trouble with Mom if I don't find that hat. . . . Well, there's no use crying. I must think. . . . If something is lost, I hear it pays to advertise. I know what I'll do. I'll sneak into the house very quietly so my mom won't know, and I'll quickly make a sign to advertise my missing hat. (*exits . . . reenters with sign*) There, this should work. (*crosses stage*) I'll just tape it over here on this fence where everyone can see it. (*crosses stage*) I'll park myself here on the porch. Oh, I think I see someone coming now.
AMANDA:	(*enters and looks at sign*) Hmmmm, what's this? (*reads aloud*) Missing, . . . a stupid hat. . . . Return to Ryan. . . . Reward!. . . Well, well, well. This is very interesting. It looks like a job for me, Amazing Amanda, child detective.
RYAN:	(*jumping up*) Are you really a detective?
AMANDA:	Absolutely!
RYAN:	Are you good at finding missing things?
AMANDA:	Oh, yes. I've found any number of lost mittens and toys. I've also found lost pets, and even a missing child or two. Who are you?
RYAN:	I am Ryan, and that's my sign you just read. Do you think you can find my hat?

AMANDA:	Probably. I'm not called Amazing Amanda for nothing.
RYAN:	Great! I'd like to hire you to do the job.
AMANDA:	Very well, but first there's the matter of pay. What's the reward?
RYAN:	I don't know. Does it have to be money? I hope not, because I don't have any money.
AMANDA:	How about chewing gum or candy? Do you have anything like that?
RYAN:	I have lollipops inside. Is that all right?
AMANDA:	Yes, I like lollipops. If I find your hat, you can give me three lollipops, one every day for three days. How's that for a deal?
RYAN:	It's a deal. Let's shake hands on it.
AMANDA:	Okay. (*They shake.*) Now, like all good detectives I have questions to ask.
RYAN:	What do you want to know?
AMANDA:	Well, first, what does this missing hat look like?
RYAN:	It's just a regular hat.
AMANDA:	A regular hat? Can't you do better than that?
RYAN:	Yes. It's a regular *stupid* hat.
AMANDA:	(*addresses audience*) I'm getting nowhere with this kid. . . .Ryan, what color is the missing *stupid* hat?
RYAN:	I forget.
AMANDA:	How could you forget?
RYAN:	Because I have more than one hat. I can't remember which one I had on today. All I know is that all of my hats are stupid-looking.
AMANDA:	Do you think you would know it if you saw it?
RYAN:	Oh, yes. I'm sure I would.
AMANDA:	Good! Now, is this missing hat lost or stolen?
RYAN:	I'm not sure.

AMANDA:	(*addresses audience*) He's not sure. Could this be a visitor from outer space? . . . Ryan, could you at least tell me where you last saw your hat?
RYAN:	Oh, yes. I can do that. (*points*) It was under that bush.
AMANDA:	That seems a funny place for a hat to be.
RYAN:	Better than on my head on a nice day like this. Anyway, I just left it there for a while. I was going to put it on before I went inside.
AMANDA:	Most people put their hats on before they go *outside*.
RYAN:	But not on a day like this . . . unless they have a mom like mine.
AMANDA:	Aha! I understand now. Your mother made you wear the hat, but you took it off.
RYAN:	I *shook* it off. Well, actually, I bent down a bit and it fell off my head. . . .
AMANDA:	. . . and you hid it under the bush and ran off to play.
RYAN:	Yes, and when I came back, it was gone. Oh! Oh! Ooooh! Am I ever in trouble!
AMANDA:	Never fear, Amanda's here! Don't go away, Ryan. I'm off to work. (*exits*)
RYAN:	It's wonderful to have Amazing Amanda working for me. There she goes like a whirlwind. I sure hope she finds that hat or I'll be grounded forever. . . . Poor me. . . . Hey, I see Amanda coming back.
AMANDA:	(*enters with baseball cap*) Ta-dah! Look what I found.
RYAN:	That's a baseball cap. It's very nice, and I wish I had one like it, but it's not my missing hat.
AMANDA:	Oh. Well, never mind, I'll try again. (*exits with cap*)

RYAN:	Let's hope she does better this time. . . . I'll soon find out. Here she comes again.
AMANDA:	(*enters with fire fighter's hat*) Look what I have here.
RYAN:	Did you find it down near the firehouse?
AMANDA:	Why, yes. How did you know?
RYAN:	Because that's a fire fighter's hat. It's not at all like mine.
AMANDA:	All right then. I'm off again. (*exits with hat*)
RYAN:	Amazing Amanda hasn't found my missing hat, but I'll say one thing for her. She's fast on her feet.
AMANDA:	(*enters with cowboy hat*) Here I am again with another hat. Isn't this a beauty?
RYAN:	It sure is. But, Amanda, it's a cowboy hat. When I grow up, I might want to be a cowboy, and then I'd love to have a hat just like that. . . . But that's *not* my missing hat.
AMANDA:	In that case, I'm on my way again. (*exits with hat*)
RYAN:	Poor Amanda! I don't think she'll ever find my hat. . . . And poor me. (*whimpers pitifully*)
AMANDA:	(*enters with pirate's hat*) I'm back again. And, Ryan, look at this beautiful, wonderful, magnificent hat.
RYAN:	That's a pirate's hat. I'm not a pirate. Wherever did you find a pirate's hat?
AMANDA:	It wasn't easy. I had to search far, far away.
RYAN:	Amanda, I don't think you will ever find my hat. You might as well give up now.
AMANDA:	Give up? Amazing Amanda doesn't give up so easily. Even if I have to go as far as the North Pole, I refuse to give up. I'm off again. (*exits with hat*)
RYAN:	This is hopeless. I might as well confess to Mom and take my punishment. . . . Oh, why didn't I just wear the stupid hat? Now I'll probably be

grounded for a month . . . or not allowed to watch TV . . . or maybe I'll get no desserts for the rest of my life. . . . Poor me. (*sobs*) . . . My goodness, I wonder where Amanda is. She must really be searching far, far away. Or maybe she decided to give up and go home. . . . Wait. . . . Way off in the distance I see someone coming. . . . Yes, it's Amanda, and she's carrying something red. . . . It must be another hat.

AMANDA: (*enters puffing with Santa's hat*) I'm back with another hat.

RYAN: Amanda! That's not my hat. That belongs to Santa Claus. You really did go to the North Pole.

AMANDA: Yes, and I'm getting tired. This is the hardest job I ever had. I think I'll rest for a while.

RYAN: First you'd better take Santa's hat right back where you found it. I 'm already in trouble with my mom. I don't want Santa Claus mad at me, too.

AMANDA: You're right. And Santa might also get mad at me, if he finds I took his hat. But you wait here, Ryan. I'm coming right back. (*exits with hat*)

RYAN: I think Amanda has finally given up, and I'm giving up, too. I might as well take down my sign. . . . (*removes sign*) I'll throw it in this trash can by the fence. (*tosses sign backstage*) There. . . . I promised I'd wait for Amanda. . . . Ah, here she is now.

AMANDA: (*enters empty-handed*) Santa's hat is back at the North Pole where it belongs.

RYAN: Good. . . . Please don't look so sad, Amanda. You did your best.

AMANDA: I really hate to give up on a job. Do you know, this is my first unsolved case. I still might think of something.

RYAN: It will have to be quick. I'm supposed to be home for lunch about now.

DOG: (*enters with Ryan's hat*) Mmmmm. Mmmmmmm.

AMANDA:	Oh, what a cute little doggie. I wonder who he belongs to.
RYAN:	He's mine. Here, Poochie! Here, boy! (*pats dog*)
AMANDA:	He seems like a very nice pet.
RYAN:	Yes, he's a good old dog.
AMANDA:	I have just one question.
RYAN:	What's that?
AMANDA:	Does he always carry a hat around with him?
RYAN:	Of course not, silly. Dogs don't do . . . Oh! . . . Oh! . . . Ooooooh!
AMANDA:	Yes, I believe that your missing hat has been found. The mystery is solved at last.
RYAN:	I can't believe it. Good old Poochie had it all along. Come here, boy, let me have it. (*takes hat from dog*)
AMANDA:	Do you know what I think?
RYAN:	No, what?
AMANDA:	I think that your dog knew that you were supposed to be wearing that hat. I'll bet he's been looking all over for you.
RYAN:	You might be right. Whatever the case, my troubles are over.
AMANDA:	I'm glad. And speaking of cases, I didn't really solve this one, so you don't owe me any reward.
RYAN:	Amanda, you worked so hard trying to help me. I'm going to pay you anyway. Come back this afternoon for the first lollipop.
AMANDA:	Okay, I'll do that. . . . And, Ryan, I don't think your hat is stupid-looking. In fact, I like it. . . . Well, good-bye for now. I'll see you later. (*exits*)
RYAN:	(*calls*) So long till this afternoon. Come on, Poochie, it's time for lunch. (*exits with hat*)
DOG:	Woof! Woof! (*exits*)

Ryan's Hat

PUPPETS: Ryan, Mom, and Amanda must be hand-action puppets in order to manipulate props. The dog should be a mouth-action puppet so that he can carry the hat.

SETTING: All of the action takes place just outside Ryan's house. The bush and fence at the opposite side of the stage are imaginary. No prop stage is necessary for the hat, which (with the puppeteer's help) can briefly rest on the frame of the puppet stage.

PROPS: The sign, with the message printed on it as described in the script, should be large enough and have the printing placed high enough so that it will be visible to the audience when it is taped to the puppet stage frame. Fresh masking tape should be attached before the performance so that the sign can be posted easily during the play. Ryan's hat can be any kind of puppet headgear that can sit easily on top of his head. A loop of sticky tape inside will keep it from falling off prematurely. If examples of the other hats cannot be found, they will have to be made. A possible simple solution would be to make two-dimensional replicas of the hats on poster board and cut them out. The audience sees each only briefly, and if the Amanda puppet holds them facing front, the audience will accept them as being real hats.

TAPING: Except for the dog's barks, sniffs, and murmurs, no special sound effects are needed for this play. Amanda's voice should be higher than Ryan's, and she should speak with authority. The mother should sound bossy.

ACTION: The puppeteer on the left should be Ryan and Mom. All of their entrances and exits should be from the side. The puppeteer on the right should operate the tape player and take the other two parts. Except for the dog's last exit when he follows Ryan, Amanda and Poochie always enter and exit at the right. The puppeteer on the right should be ready to help secure the sign and to see that Ryan's hat shakes off at the right time and remains in audience view. When Ryan disposes of the sign, he can simply drop it backstage.

TIME: 14 minutes. Allow extra time for introductory music.

VEGETABLES

CHARACTERS

MAMA
MATTHEW
DR. CHOW

PROPS

PICTURES OF PEAS,
GREEN BEANS,
BEETS,
BROCCOLI,
CARROTS,
SPINACH, AND
ZUCCHINI

MAMA: (*enters and addresses audience*)

I have a son named Matthew, a most delightful
    boy.
Except for one small problem, he is his mama's
    joy.
But he won't eat his vegetables. They are not in
    his diet,
Although I serve them every day, and beg him,
    Matthew, try it.
Asparagus to zucchini, everything from A to Z,
He hates them all, and this has been an awful
    trial to me.
Served raw to him in salad? Dull, he says, and
    pallid.
Cooked? Even worse. Call the doctor! Call the
    nurse!
Just stick around a moment, and I'll show you
    what I mean,
And why I've asked an expert to the house to
    intervene.
(*calls*) Matthew, Matthew, please come here.
    We must discuss your dinner, dear. . . .

MATTHEW:	(*enters*) Here I am, but let's not fuss.
	There is nothing to discuss.
	You know, Mama, that I hate
	Veg-e-tables on my plate.
	Nasty things, they make me gag.
	It won't do any good to nag. . . .
MAMA:	I've given up on nagging, son. I know it does no good.
	A new approach is called for. You'll soon eat what you should.
	A visitor is coming, a child psychologist,
	Who also, as it happens, is a skillful hypnotist.
	Disorders like yours, Matthew, are duck soup to Dr. Chow.
	Food problems are his specialty. Ah, here's the doctor now. . . .
DR. CHOW:	(*enters*) I'm Dr. Chow. How do you do? (*bows*)
	How may I be of help to you?
MAMA:	Ah, Doctor, this is Matthew, my veggie-hating child.
	That he won't even taste them is about to drive me wild.
	It really was my last resort to call someone like you.
	I hope, since you're a specialist, there's something you can do. . . .
DR. CHOW:	Yes, dear lady, never fear,
	Now that Dr. Chow is here. . . .
	Matthew, Matthew, please draw near.
	I have a question for your ear. . . .
	(*Matthew draws near.*)
	Vegetables, there are so many.
	Do you mean you won't eat *any*?. . . .
MATTHEW:	Well, I'll eat potatoes, and sometimes tomatoes,
	And often a nice ear of corn.
	But, as for the rest, they can't pass the test.
	I've hated them since I was born.
DR. CHOW:	Well, bless your heart! At least that's a start.

And, as for the rest, they'll soon pass the test.
Look into my eyes, as I hypnotize.

(*stares into Matthew's eyes*)

Matthew, . . . Matthew, . . . Matthew, . . . go to
sleep awhile,
And soon, when you see vegetables, you'll nod
your head and smile.
I'll be showing you some pictures of the very
things you hate,
When I clap my hands you'll change your mind
and really think they're great.
Now, when you see each picture, tell me what
you think.
Then, clappity-clap, you will change, quick as a
wink. . . .

MATTHEW: (*looking at picture of peas that pops up*)

Peas look like marbles for an elf,
Not food for children like myself.

(*Dr. Chow claps*)

An elf I'll be, so let's begin
That game. I'll shoot those marbles in. . . .

(*picture of green beans pops up replacing first picture*)

Green beans I really hate,
Caterpillars on my plate.

(*Dr. Chow claps*)

But I'm a birdie. Here I come,
And I will eat them. Yum, yum, yum! . . .

(*picture of beets pops up*)

Beets! They're boring. Nothing's duller,
Although red's my favorite color.

(*Dr. Chow claps*)

I'll be an artist. So, instead
Of beets, I'll eat the color red. . . .

(*picture of broccoli pops up*)

Broccoli looks like a tree,
Not food for little kids like me.

(*Dr. Chow claps*)

But that tree looks like tasty wood.
A broccoli forest might be good. . . .

(*picture of carrots pops up*)

Carrots, if the truth be told,
Are horrid, though they look like gold.

(*Dr. Chow claps*)

I'll be King Midas. Give me lots
Of golden carrots, pots and pots. . . .

(*picture of spinach pops up*)

Spinach! What a thing to feed
A child. I'd rather eat a weed.

(*Dr. Chow claps*)

But, just like Popeye, watch me hustle,
Eat it up, and make a muscle. . . .

(*picture of zucchini pops up*)

Zucchini, I am very sure,
Is only fit for a dinosaur.

(*Dr. Chow claps*)

A brontosaurus? Yes, that's me.
I'll eat zucchini—one, two, three. . . .

DR. CHOW: (*turning to Mama and bowing*)

Madam, I am finished, and I am sure you'll find
That the child who hated vegetables has had a
change of mind.
I shall wake him in a moment. Then, dear lady,
be advised
To ask him what he'd like to eat. I think you'll
be surprised.

(*turning to Matthew*)

Matthew, . . . Matthew, . . . Matthew, . . . we're
done with pictures now.
I'll clap. Then you'll wake up and wave good-bye
to Dr. Chow.

(*Dr. Chow claps, bows, and waves to Matthew who
waves back . . . Dr. Chow bows again and exits*) . . .

MATTHEW: I feel as if I've had a nap.
Did I just hear somebody clap? . . .

MAMA: Yes, Matthew, that was Dr. Chow.
But it is time for dinner now,
And I think you deserve a treat,
So tell me what you'd like to eat. . . .

MATTHEW: I'm really starved. Now let me see. . . .
What food would taste the best to me?
Ah, yes, . . . and I confess, . . . I would like rather
more than less
Of carrots, zucchini, or onions with peas,
Or maybe some green beans or broccoli, please.
A salad or cole slaw, and I will confide
That I'd like some spinach with beets on the
side,
Artichokes, cauliflower, turnips, tomatoes,
Celery, radishes, lots of potatoes!
Some corn on the cob would certainly do,
And I might even relish a parsnip or two,
Or maybe asparagus—that would taste good—
Or, . . . just give me samples of each, if you
would. . . .

MAMA: This has been a miracle, thanks to Dr. Chow.

I'll give you everything you want. I'll start the cooking now,

And after all those vegetables, it really wouldn't hurt

To end with something frivolous, so what about dessert?

MATTHEW: Dessert? . . . Oh, I couldn't. . . . I wouldn't. . . . I shouldn't. . . .

MAMA: No sweet? . . . No treat? . . . The change is complete! . . .

I must get busy, Matthew. To the kitchen I will go.

If you decide you want dessert, be sure to let me know.

. . . (*turns to leave*)

MATTHEW: Oh, Mama, Mama, I just though of something I might try.

MAMA: Wonderful! What is it, dear? . . .

MATTHEW: . . . Sweet potato pie!

Vegetables

PUPPETS: Although the stage directions indicate that Matthew waves to Dr. Chow, this action is not essential to the play, so Matthew can be either hand- or mouth-action. The same applies to Mama, who only speaks. Dr. Chow is required to clap, so he must be a hand-action puppet. The name, Chow, was chosen as a pun to indicate that the character is concerned with food and eating, but it would be fitting and compatible with his formal manners if Dr. Chow resembled a Chinese gentleman.

PROPS: Each vegetable should be boldly drawn in color on a square large enough (7″ × 8″ suggested) for the audience to identify. The names may be printed on them, too. Each picture should be attached to an ice cream stick so that it can be held up for viewing. Numbering the pictures in back will ensure that they are displayed in the proper order.

TAPING: Timing is very important, so the ellipses used to indicate pauses must be carefully observed. The voices should be different pitches, Dr. Chow's being the lowest. Several practice run-throughs would be a good idea so that the right words are emphasized during recording. Although in verse, the sentiments should be expressed naturally, not in a singsong way. The only sound effect is Dr. Chow's clapping. This should be done by the person who records Matthew's voice, since all except the final clap occur during his long speech.

ACTION: The puppeteer on the left should be Mama and
            Matthew, and both characters enter from the left.
            The puppeteer on the right should operate the
            tape player and be Dr. Chow, who enters and exits
            right. This puppeteer should also hold up the
            vegetable pictures in the correct order when
            needed. Dr. Chow can raise his arm in the direc-
            tion of each vegetable as it appears and must
            remember to clap in synchrony with the tape.
            Mama should move aside while Matthew is being
            hypnotized by Dr. Chow, which must be at close
            range. The end of the play is very abrupt, so the
            two puppets can hug, pat, etc. (or, if mouth-action
            puppets, laugh) before bowing and exiting left.

TIME: 7 $^1/_2$ minutes. Allow extra time for introductory
            music.

A NEW PUNCH AND JUDY

CHARACTERS

PUNCH
JUDY
BABY
CLOWN
TEACHER
TOBY (A DOG)
DOCTOR
POLICEMAN
CROCODILE

PROPS

FEATHER DUSTER
FEATHER
RULER
HANDCUFFS

	(*off-stage sound of "Pop Goes the Weasel" played on the kazoo*)
PUNCH:	(*enters and addresses audience*)
	Root-i-toot-toot! Root-i-toot-toot! I'm Mr. Punch. Do you think me cute? If you think me cute, I hope you'll stay To watch our merry little play. . . .
	Ah, no one is leaving, I see. Good! *You* are about to get your first reward, because *I* am about to introduce you to my bee-yoo-tiful wife. If you think I'm handsome, just wait till you see her. (*calls*) Judy! Judy! Judy! Where are you, my love?
JUDY:	(*enters with feather duster*) Where do you think I am, old sausage nose? I'm inside doing my housework, as usual. Work! Work! Work!
PUNCH:	Oh, dearie me! What a shame! I would so like some company.

JUDY: Good! I'll get you some company. Just wait here. (*exits*)

PUNCH: Some company, she says. Goody-goody! Good! Good! Good!

JUDY: (*enters with baby*) Here's some company for you. You can sit the baby while I work. Here, take him. (*gives baby to Punch and exits*)

PUNCH: And for finer company a proud father could not ask. What a pretty child he is! Looks just like me, he does.

BABY: (*screams*) Wahhh. . . . Wahhhhh. . . .

PUNCH: (*sings*) Rockabye, baby. Don't be so bad. If you don't stop bawling, you'll wish that you had.

BABY: Wahhhh. . . . Wahhhhh. . . .

PUNCH: There, there. Good boy! (*asks audience*) Did you ever see a sweeter child, or a prettier one? He has my nose.

BABY: (*grabbing Punch's nose*) Wahhhh. . . Wahhhhhh. . . .

PUNCH: Oh! Ow! Now he really has my nose. Let go. Let go, I say. I'll shake you loose, you rascal, you. (*shakes head violently*)

BABY: Wahhhhhh. . . . (*exits, screams fading as he falls backstage*)

PUNCH: (*rubbing nose*) That wasn't the kind of company I had in mind. Ah, here comes my good Judy again.

JUDY: (*enters with duster*) Shame on you, Punch. How dare you throw our baby out the window?

PUNCH: I didn't throw him. He jumped.

JUDY: Well, I caught him.

PUNCH: I thought you might be lurking below. So all is well.

JUDY: Lucky for you.

PUNCH: I'm tickled pink.

JUDY: I'll tickle you, you old rogue. (*shakes duster in his face*) Here! Take that!

PUNCH: (*sneezing loudly*) A mighty weapon! It spits dust straight up my poor nose.

JUDY: Here's some more dust for your nose. (*shakes duster in his face*) Take that, and that!

PUNCH: (*sneezes*) A fine weapon, and one that I shall make my own. (*snatches duster and shakes it in Judy's face*) There! Take that, and that!

JUDY: (*sneezes*) Give me my duster.

PUNCH: I'll give it to you. (*shakes duster in her face*) Take that!

JUDY: Stop! Stop! Stop! (*sneezes*) Ah-choo. . . . Ah-choo. . . . Ah-Ah-choo. . . . (*exits, sinking from sight*)

PUNCH: (*dancing*) Root-i-toot-toot! Root-i-toot-toot!
           A bit of dust is good for the snoot.

CLOWN: (*enters with feather*) Ha-ha-ha-ha-ha.

PUNCH: And what's so funny, if I may ask?

CLOWN: You may ask, and I shall answer. I am a clown, a jolly clown, a happy clown, a merry clown, a joyful clown, a. . .

PUNCH: A blabbermouth clown. Enough! Enough! I can see what you are, but why do you laugh? Could it be my wonderful nose you find laughable?

CLOWN: Oh, no, sir. Your nose is magnificent. I laugh because I am jolly, as all good clowns should be.

PUNCH: But you carry a weapon. I think you mean to harm me.

CLOWN:	Oh, no, sir. My feather is only for tickling.
PUNCH:	Well, then, tickle me.
CLOWN:	I'd rather not.
PUNCH:	I insist.
CLOWN:	Oh, very well. I'll give a light tickle to your wonderful nose. (*tickles Punch's nose*)
PUNCH:	Aha! You attacked me, and I shall defend myself. How do you like these tickles? (*flourishes duster in clown's face*)
CLOWN:	(*sneezes*) Help! Help! . . . (*exits*)
PUNCH:	(*dancing*) Root-i-toot-toot! When said and done, Many feathers are better than one.
TEACHER:	(*enters with ruler*) Punch, you naughty boy!
PUNCH:	Boy? Madam, where are your eyes? I am a man.
TEACHER:	A man in size perhaps, but still a boy to me.
PUNCH:	Oh, no! It's Miss Grumpy, my old, old, old, old teacher, mean as ever, and still with her ruler!
TEACHER:	I'll never be too old to rap your knuckles, you naughty boy.
PUNCH:	But I was always so good. Surely you remember how nicely I clapped the erasers for you.
TEACHER:	Yes, but you always clapped them right under my nose where I could taste the dust. Come here, naughty boy. I shall rap your knuckles again as I did so often in the past. (*swings ruler, missing*)
PUNCH:	But not before you taste more dust. (*shakes duster in her face*)
TEACHER:	(*sneezes*) Naughty boy! Naughty boy! Naughty bo-o-o-y! (*exits*)
PUNCH:	(*dancing*) Root-i-toot, and away! Good riddance, I say. (*addresses audience*) Have you ever seen meaner,

nastier folk than those you've met today? They mean me harm, they do, and I'm such a pussycat of a fellow. (*sings*) I'm such a pussycat, sweet little pussycat, dear little pussycat, me . . .

TOBY: (*enters*) Woof! Woof!

PUNCH: Oh, it's Toby, my fine little dog. He's come to see his pussycat of a master, he has. Here, Toby. Let me give you a pat.

TOBY: Grrrrrrr. . . .

PUNCH: And he's so sweet-tempered!

TOBY: Woof! Woof! Grrrrr. (*bites Punch's nose*)

PUNCH: Ow! Ow! My poor nose! Ungrateful beast! (*swings duster at Toby*)

TOBY: Yip! Yip! Yip! (*exits*)

PUNCH: Help! Help! Doctor! Doctor! I am dying. (*lies down*)

DOCTOR: (*enters*) You called for me?

PUNCH: Yes, dear doctor. And now it's you that's calling, as all good doctors should.

DOCTOR: And what is hurting? (*bends over Punch*)

PUNCH: My nose. My nose is killing me.

DOCTOR: Then your nose should be punished. (*hits Punch's nose*) There! I have cured you.

PUNCH: (*jumping up*) And I will pay you for making me well. (*shakes duster in doctor's face*) How's that for pay?

DOCTOR: (*sneezes*) Murder! Murder! Help! Police! (*exits*)

POLICEMAN: (*enters with handcuffs*) Where is he? Where is the murderer?

PUNCH: He went that way. (*points*)

POLICEMAN: Then, never mind. I will catch him later. Tell me, sir, where is the victim? Who is killed?

PUNCH:	My nose is the victim. Just look at it.
POLICEMAN:	(*looks*) It does not look dead to me.
PUNCH:	Well, look more closely. (*pokes nose into policeman's face*)
POLICEMAN:	Get your nose out of my face.
PUNCH:	Get your face out of my nose.
POLICEMAN:	Oh, you are a bad one. It's off to jail for you. Come here at once. I will handcuff your wrist to mine.
PUNCH:	(*looking*) Handcuffs? Oh, let me see. Show me how they work.
POLICEMAN:	It's simple. The bracelet fits over the wrist, like this. (*puts his own hand into the cuff*) See, it fits me, and it will fit you, too. Then, click-click, it snaps shut, like this. . . . Oh, no! I am caught in my own handcuffs. How's that for a pickle?
PUNCH:	And how's this for a tickle? (*shakes duster in policeman's face*)
POLICEMAN:	Oh, no, no, no, no, noooooo. . . (*exits*)
PUNCH:	(*dancing*) Root-i-toot-toot! Marvelous me! He goes to jail, and I go free.
	Ah, who comes now? It looks to be a walking suitcase, or perhaps a crocodile, which is much the same thing.
CROCODILE:	(*enters*) Lunch. . . . Lunch. . . .
PUNCH:	No, no! I'm Punch. . . . Punch. . . .
CROCODILE:	You may be Punch to you, but you're lunch to me.
PUNCH:	Monster! You mean to nip my nose.
CROCODILE:	I mean to nip all of you.
PUNCH:	Not while I have my wonderful weapon. (*shakes duster in crocodile's face*) How do you like that?

CROCODILE:	It will be all right for a first course. (*snaps mouth shut on duster, and they tug back and forth*)
PUNCH:	No! No! Let go, you fiend. (*they tug and thrash*)
CROCODILE:	Rrrrrrrrr. . . .
PUNCH:	Let go!. . . . Ooops! (*crocodile pulls duster below stage and pops back up*) Awrrr, the monster has swallowed my wonderful weapon.
CROCODILE:	And now for the rest of my lunch. . . .
PUNCH:	Help! Help! (*crocodile pulls Punch below*) . . . Ooooh, I am eaten! The beast has swallowed me whole.
CROCODILE:	(*enters*) Very tasty, too, but a bit heavy in my belly.
PUNCH:	(*from offstage*) Let me out. Let me out, I say. I'll make you sorry, I will. Just wait.
CROCODILE:	My lunch speaks to me. Being swallowed whole did not shut his mouth.
PUNCH:	(*from offstage*) I warned you. Now I have found my weapon. How do you like this? Tickle, tickle, tickle, tickle. . . .
CROCODILE:	Ha-ha-ha-ha-ha. . . . Ho-ho-ho-ho-ho-ho-ho. . . . (*sinks from sight*) Ah-choo! . . . Ah-choo! . . . Ah-choooooo . . .
PUNCH:	(*enters, flying up from below and clutching duster*) Ta-dah!
	(*dancing*) Root-it-toot-toot! And toodle-oo, For I must say good-bye to you. That's the end of our little play, And Mr. Punch has won the day!
	(*bows and exits as crocodile rises, jaws snapping, to chase him offstage*)

A New Punch and Judy

Production notes

NOTE:
This is a laundered version of the bawdy, violent Punch-and-Judy shows of nineteenth-century England in which a variety of characters met death at Punch's hands. Here, a feather duster snatched from Judy replaces the hero's lethal stick. Fits of dust induced sneezing substitute for the slaying, and rather than tricking the hangman to hang himself, Punch tricks the policeman into handcuffing himself. The schoolteacher was invented for this play, replacing several traditional authority figures.

PUPPETS:
All of the people puppets should be the hand-action variety. While the title characters need not have their traditional stylized humps, Punch, Judy, and their baby should be "grotesque with large hooked noses and jutting chins. Papier-mâché is suggested as a substitute for carved wooden heads. Punch's costume should be red-trimmed with yellow, and his cap should be pointed. Judy should wear a mobcap, and the baby a bonnet. The other people puppets need not have grotesque features, but should be costumed in a manner that suggests their vocations. Toby can be any mouth-action dog puppet. The crocodile should be green and have a large mouth in order to (believably) drag Punch below to swallow.

PROPS:
Judy's duster should be made of fluffy feathers securely attached to a dowel handle. The clown's

single feather should be large enough for easy visibility. A six-inch ruler is suggested for the teacher. The handcuffs can be made of heavy silver paper, foil-wrapped cardboard, or even two tiny tuna cans wired together.

TAPING:

Punch's voice should be rasping and squeaky, and Judy's an even higher squeak. The baby's bawling should be shrill. The other voices can be more ordinary in sound and pitch, the crocodile's being lowest and slowest. A clicking noise would suggest the snapping shut of handcuffs. Regarding music, any member of the recording cast who knows the tune can hum "Pop Goes the Weasel" through the kazoo, and slightly off-key is all right. Punch's version of "Rockabye, Baby" should be sung to the traditional melody. The few bars of his pussycat song should be sung to the tune of "I'm Called Little Buttercup" from Gilbert and Sullivan's *H.M.S. Pinafore*. It is very important to observe pauses for stage business while taping, especially when Punch wrestles with the crocodile.

ACTION:

The puppeteer on the right should be Punch and the baby, and the puppeteer on the left should operate the tape player and be all of the other characters. In keeping with Punch tradition (in which itinerant puppeteers worked in narrow, enclosed booths) entrances and exits should be made from below, the characters popping up and down according to the script. The one exception is at the end when Punch (after rising for a bow) can exit right, followed by the crocodile. Several of the props can be attached to their puppets' hands: the feather (lightweight) to one of the clown's hands; the ruler (heavier) to both of the teacher's hands; and a handcuff over one of the policeman's wrists. When the script calls for the policeman to handcuff himself, the

remaining bracelet can be slipped over his other
hand.

TIME: 12 $^1/_2$ minutes. This includes the hummed chorus
of "Pop Goes the Weasel." No other introductory
music is suggested.

EXERCISE TIME

CHARACTER*

MISSY MUSCLE

MISSY MUSCLE: (*enters, jogging*) Hello, boys and girls. My name is Melissa, but you can call me Missy Muscle. I've said hello to you, and I've told you my name. Now it's your turn to greet me. I'd like to hear you say, "Hello, Missy Muscle." (*waits*) . . . Now, if you try that again, I'll say it with you. . . . "Hello, Missy Muscle!" . . . Good! . . . I can see that some of you are wiggle worms, so I thought you might like to get the wiggles out. So stand up, everyone. It's EXERCISE TIME! Watch me and do everything I do. . . . (*demonstrates*) First bend as far as you can this way. . . . Now bend as far as you can the other way. . . . Now we'll bend like that from side to side while I count. . . . One . . . two . . . one . . . two . . . one . . . two . . . one . . . two . . . one . . . two . . . one . . . two . . . one . . . two . . . one . . . two. . . . Now we'll do some twists. Twist as far as you can this way. . . . Now twist as far as you can the other way. . . . I will count. . . . One . . . two . . . one . . . two . . . one . . . two . . . one . . . two . . . one . . . two . . . one . . . two . . . one . . . two . . . one . . . two. . . Now we'll touch toes like this. . . . Down . . . up . . . down . . . up . . . down . . . up . . . down . . . up . . . down . . . up . . . down . . . up . . . down . . . up. . . . Now

*The voice of Missy Muscle is also used in the play, "Couch Potatoes."

180

for some jumps. Let's do them together. . . . Jump, jump, jump, jump, jump, jump, jump!. . . Oh, that was fun! I always feel so good when I exercise. I hope you do, too. Now that the wiggles are out of your systems, I hope you feel like sitting down again, because there's more fun in store for you. I may see you later. Good-bye for now. (*exits, jogging and waving*)

Exercise Time

Production notes

PUPPET:

Missy Muscle, the only puppet needed for this audience participation piece, should be a small, flexible hand-action puppet. Her head should fit the puppeteer's finger snugly so that it doesn't come loose when she touches her toes. Although, of course, she does not have legs, her costume should in some way suggest the exercise attire of a television aerobics instructor.

TAPING:

Whoever records the voice of Missy Muscle should visualize the exercises that will be demonstrated so that the timing will be right. If this piece is used in the same program as "Couch Potatoes," the voice of Missy Muscle should be the same.

ACTION:

Only one puppeteer is needed for this show. Since all of the exercises are described by the character, the puppeteer need only listen to the tape to do everything necessary.

TIME:

2 $^1/_2$ minutes.

THROW IT IN THE LITTER BIN

CHARACTERS*

SUSIE
BRYAN

PROP

SIGN

(*Susie and Bryan enter from opposite sides*)

SUSIE:	Hi, Bryan.
BRYAN:	Hi, Susie.
SUSIE:	Guess what we talked about in school today.
BRYAN:	Do I have to guess?
SUSIE:	Sure, give it a try.
BRYAN:	Holidays! You talked about which one is the most fun.
SUSIE:	No, that's not it.
BRYAN:	You talked about arithmetic, how to add six and seven without taking your shoes and socks off.
SUSIE:	No, silly, that's not it.
BRYAN:	You talked about movies . . . or pets . . . or fairy tales.
SUSIE:	No . . . no . . . and no.
BRYAN:	Well, I give up. What *did* you talk about?
SUSIE:	Littering. We talked about littering. And do you know what my teacher, Ms. Watch-yer-step, said?
BRYAN:	No, I don't. Do I have to guess?

*Susie and Bryan are also characters in the play, "Litterbugs."

183

SUSIE: No, I'll tell you. She said that most of the litter on sidewalks and streets comes from people throwing down cans or boxes or bottles or pieces of paper after they've finished eating or drinking something.

BRYAN: I guess that's right.

SUSIE: She said that people should dispose of this trash properly.

BRYAN: I know. I'll bet she told you to throw that kind of stuff in the trash can.

SUSIE: Oh, Ms. Watch-yer-step was much fancier and classier than that. She said, (*imitates teacher's voice*) "Throw it in the litter bin!"

BRYAN: That's definitely fancier *and* classier.

SUSIE: So we have a special school project. . . . Stories, posters, maybe even a puppet play.

BRYAN: Like this one, right?

SUSIE: Right! Everyone in the class has to do something.

BRYAN: What are you going to do?

SUSIE: I've already done it. Right after school I ran home and wrote a poem. But I need help to put it across. Will you help me?

BRYAN: Sure, but what do I have to do?

SUSIE: When I clap my hands, you say, "Throw it in the litter bin."

BRYAN: That sounds easy.

SUSIE: Come to think of it, I can use more help than just one person. (*leans forward to address audience*) Please, you kids out there, will you help, too? (*waits for response*) . . . All right, this is how to do it. Whenever I clap my hands, Bryan will say, "Throw it in the litter bin," and I want you to say it, too. Let's get on with it. Bryan, are you ready?

BRYAN: Yes, I'm ready.

SUSIE: (*craning at audience*) Kids, are you ready, too? (*waits for response*) . . . It's up to you to help Bryan. Well, here we go! (*Susie and Bryan sway side to side as they recite*)

Your fries and burger tasted grand.
The empty box is in your hand.
Don't toss it in the air to spin. (*claps*)

BRYAN: Throw it in the litter bin.

SUSIE: A wrapper from a candy bar
Just flung away will not go far.
So, putting on your sweetest grin, (*claps*)

BRYAN: Throw it in the litter bin.

SUSIE: The napkin from your pizza slice
Is all that's left, so please be nice.
Use it to wipe your greasy chin, Then, (*claps*)

BRYAN: Throw it in the litter bin.

SUSIE: Ice cream and lollipops are kicks,
But when they're gone, you're left with sticks.
Pretend your stick's a javelin. (*claps*)

BRYAN: Throw it in the litter bin.

SUSIE: Some parts of fruit are good, some not,
But on the ground, what's left will rot.
So, apple core? Banana skin? (*claps*)

BRYAN: Throw it in the litter bin.

SUSIE: You've drunk some soda pop outside,
But something's left you cannot hide.
Plastic, glass, or maybe tin, (*claps*)

BRYAN: Throw it in the litter bin.

SUSIE: Some things can be recycled, too.
If you can do that, good for you!
But if you can't, you still can win. (*claps*)

BRYAN: Throw it in the litter bin. . . .

SUSIE: Well, that's it. What do you think?

BRYAN:	Oh, Susie, I like it! I'll bet Ms. Watch-yer-step will give you an A.
SUSIE:	Well, I don't know. After all, it's just a bunch of words, and my teacher is always saying that I talk too much. She even sent a note home to my mother.
BRYAN:	Oh, yes, I remember that.
SUSIE:	So, just in case she doesn't like it, I did something else, too. I'm not very good in art—words are *my* thing—but I made a sign to put up in front of the school.
BRYAN:	You made a sign? Where is it?
SUSIE:	In my house. Wait here just a minute. (*exits and returns dragging sign*) . . . Here it is.
BRYAN:	If you don't hold it up, nobody can see it. What does it say?
SUSIE:	Can't you guess? Here take a good look. (*holds sign so that Bryan and then the audience can read it*)
BOTH:	Throw it in the litter bin!

Throw It in the Litter Bin*

Production notes

PUPPETS: Although words are more important than action to this play, Susie is required to clap her hands and carry a sign, so both the boy and girl should be hand-action puppets. They should be compatible in size and appearance.

PROP: The sign, poster board glued to an ice cream stick, should be large enough so that the audience can read THROW IT IN THE LITTER BIN. The printing should be amateurish, and a simple squiggly border will be enough decoration.

TAPING: Since this play is essentially a dialogue, the two voices should be different in pitch. Practice is advised, especially for the rap poem. Attention to the cadence and clear enunciation are essential. Susie's clapping should be recorded.

ACTION: The action is so simple that reading the play will suffice for rehearsal. The puppets enter from opposite sides and remain center stage until Susie exits to get her sign. They should sway rhythmically as they recite, each standing very still as the other speaks.

TIME: 5 minutes.

---

*In the interests of ecology, the first draft of this play (like the others in this book) was written on the backs of outdated library replacement lists and flyers.

IN-THE-MIDDLE-TIME

CHARACTERS

TONY
BEAR

TONY:	(*enters, bows, and addresses audience*) Hello, girls and boys. I hope you enjoyed the play you just saw. Our program isn't over yet, though, so don't go away. The puppets are backstage putting on their costumes for another play. They'll be ready shortly. But, meanwhile, it's intermission time.
BEAR:	(*enters*) What? What did you say?
TONY:	I said it's intermission time.
BEAR:	Oh, yes. That's what I thought you said, in-ter-mis-sion time.
TONY:	So? Anything else?
BEAR:	Uh, yes.
TONY:	Well, what?
BEAR:	I . . . uh . . . hate to ask, but what does in-ter-mis-sion mean?
TONY:	The intermission is the time between the acts of a play, or in some cases, between two plays. It's the time-out period right in the middle.
BEAR:	I see. . . . Then why don't you call it in-the-middle time?
TONY:	Because everyone calls it intermission.
BEAR:	I like in-the-middle better.

TONY:	I don't care what you like. . . Who *are* you anyway?
BEAR:	I am Bear, Theodore Edward Bear, actually. But that's such a long name, so most folks call me Ted E. for short, Ted . . . E. . . . Bear.
TONY:	Teddy Bear?
BEAR:	Well, I guess that's right, if you say it real fast. Really, though, I'm just an ordinary bear. But you can call me Teddy if you like. It does sound kind of nice and friendly and cuddly.
TONY:	I'm not here to cuddle you, so I'll just call you Bear.
BEAR:	That's fine with me. And, by the way, if I might be so bold as to ask, what is your name?
TONY:	Oh, I'm Anthony Algernon Abercrombie, but, like you, I have a nickname. Everyone calls me Tony. I came out here today to announce the intermission.
BEAR:	In-the-middle.
TONY:	All right, in-the-middle. What I'm saying is that *I* have a reason to be here, Bear. But why are *you* out here on this puppet stage? Is there anything you want?
BEAR:	Well, Tony, since you asked, I'd like to know what these boys and girls are going to do during their in-the-middle time.
TONY:	Nothing special. They can just hang around till we're ready to go on again.
BEAR:	But that's boring. . . . Booorrr-ing.
TONY:	They can get up and stretch or walk around if they like. That would be fine.
BEAR:	Humph.
TONY:	I can tell you don't like that idea. Well, then, what would you suggest?

BEAR:	I know a game.
TONY:	We don't have time for games.
BEAR:	This is just a short one. The kids can not only move about, but they'll have a bit of fun while they're doing it, and then they'll be ready to sit still during the next play.
TONY:	All right, I'm convinced. That's a good idea. We'll play the game, but you'll have to tell us what to do.
BEAR:	I'll be glad to. You kids have to listen to me and do what I say, but only when you're supposed to do it. That goes for you, too, Tony.
TONY:	Okay.
BEAR:	Stand up, everyone. . . . On your feet! On your feet! . . . Are you ready for our game? . . . Fine! . . . How about you, Tony?
TONY:	I'm ready.
BEAR:	First, I want you all to check on what you're wearing. Do you have anything on that's red? If you do, nod your head. Keep nodding. . . . Up and down. . . . Up and down. . . . Keep going until I tell you to stop. . . . I see Tony nodding. He has on a red tie.. . . All right, now you can stop. . . . Next, if you have on something blue, flap your arms. . . . Come on, flap them hard. . . . Harder. . . . You can do better than that. Flap those arms. . . . Don't stop yet. . . . All right, *now* you can stop. Now, who is wearing jeans with a T-shirt or any kind of sweats? I want all of you people to turn around in a circle. . . . Again. . . . Again. . . . Once more. . . . Hey, kids, you'd better stop now. . . . I don't want you to get dizzy. . . . Let's see, what should we do next? . . . Oh, I know! Is anyone wearing sneakers or shoes good for running? If you are, show me how they work. Jog in place. . . . Jog, jog, jog, jog, jog, jog, jog, jog, jog. . . . Keep jogging. . . . Jog, jog, jog, jog, jog, jog, jog, jog, jog. . . .

Okay, now you can stop. . . . I think it's time to try something different.

TONY: Yes, you must be running out of clothes to talk about.

BEAR: Oh, I know what to ask next. . . . Who has a sibling at home?. . . . Do I see some puzzled faces? Sibling is a word I learned last week. It means sister or brother. . . . So if you have a sister or brother at home, swing your arms from side to side. . . . Come on now, swing them hard . . . side to side . . . to and fro . . . hither and yon . . . Beautiful!. . . . Now stop! I saw old Tony swinging his arms. What sibling do you have, Tony?

TONY: I have a little brother at home, and, boy, is he a pest!

BEAR: Little brothers are supposed to be that way. It's the law.

TONY: What next?

BEAR: I've thought of something really special. I want all of you boys out there to jump for joy. Just the boys now. Come on, boys, jump . . . jump . . . jump . . . jump. Jump for joy, because you're a boy. . . . Jump . . . jump . . . jump . . . jump. . . . Stop! Stop!. . . Now it's the girls turn. Come on, girls, jump . . . jump . . . jump . . . jump. Jump for joy, because you're *not* a boy. . . . Jump . . . jump . . . jump . . . jump. . . .

TONY: Bear! Bear! Is your game almost over? It's time for the puppet play.

BEAR: There's just one more thing. I want to know who likes ice cream. I want everyone who likes ice cream to sit down.

TONY: But everyone likes ice cream.

BEAR: I know. I was being clever. . . . If any of you out there are still standing, that means you hate ice cream. . . . See, now everyone is sitting down again. They're all ready for the play to begin.

TONY: That *was* clever, Bear, and it was a most exciting intermission.

BEAR: In-the-middle, Tony. In-the-middle.

TONY: Whatever. (*exits*)

BEAR: (*addresses audience*) *You* know and *I* know that it really should be in-the-middle, don't we? (*exits*)

In-The-Middle Time

Production notes

PUPPETS: Tony should be a hand-action puppet. His costume should include a red tie of some kind, since this is mentioned in the script. Bear should be a mouth-action puppet.

TAPING: Both are male characters, but their voices should be noticeably different. Bear should speak slowly and enunciate carefully in a deeper, slightly louder voice that will be heard while the audience is moving about. The pauses during this action must be carefully observed, since small children do not respond quickly to fast-paced verbal directions. The person recording Bear's role should visualize the audience participation during the taping.

ACTION: The action is very simple. Entrances may be made from either side, and once on stage, the characters remain in place until they exit. During Bear's game, Tony moves only when the description pertains to him—red tie, having a sibling, being a boy, and (possibly) wearing blue. Since he cannot turn around, does not wear jeans, T-shirt, or sweats, and is not a girl, it will be easy for the puppeteer to remember that he must stand very still during these segments. Since the audience cannot see that he lacks feet (and therefore shoes of any kind), he could seem to jog when that is mentioned. To encourage participation, a female assistant wearing everything described in the script could stand by the puppet stage to demon-

strate the moves while urging the children to
move in time with taped commands. Like Tony,
she should stand still when something does not
pertain to her, in this case, only the boys' segment.

TIME: 8 minutes. Since this audience participation piece
functions as an intermission (in-the-middle), it
should be used between two regular puppet plays.
It is not necessary to allow any extra time for
introductory music.

LET'S BE PUPPETS

CHARACTERS	PROPS
BRENT	FOAM BALLS*
BRUTUS, A DOG	

ACT 1

BRENT: *(enters and addresses audience)* Hello, everybody. My name is Brent, and I am a hand puppet. I am also an actor by profession. Yes, it's my regular job to appear in puppet plays. With some help from people behind the scenes, I can do all sorts of things. Let me tell you about some of them. Better still, let me show you. Watch and listen. *(demonstrates as described)* Of course, I can move about very well. I can creep across the stage, like this . . . slowly . . . slowly. . . . Or I can seem to skip, like this . . . or perhaps run very fast . . . or even slide, like this. . . . Wheeeeeeeee! Ooops! *(falls and speaks from prone position)* If I fall down, don't worry. I can stand right back up. *(stands)* See, I'm good as new. If my part calls for me to be a ghost, or a witch, or maybe a bird, I can even appear to float or fly, like this . . . to one side . . . or the other. . . . Of course, if I'm onstage by myself, I usually like to stay right here in the middle. . . . I can do other things, too. I can pick up props and carry them about, but only if I use both hands. I will show you. *(picks up*

*Optional for audience participation: Act 2, Conclusion 2

195

imaginary prop) Oh, this is heavy! I'd better put it down. . . . There, that's better. . . .If I hear music, I can dance, like this. (*sings while dancing*) Old MacDonald had a farm, E-I-E-I-O. . . . And I can clap my hands in time to music, too. (*sings while clapping*) Twinkle, twinkle, little star, how I wonder what you are! . . . And I've already shown you how beautifully I can sing. People enjoy my songs, even if my lips don't move while I'm singing. Something I can do 'specially well is to wave at you in the audience. I love to wave, like this. . . .Hi, out there! Of course, there are some things I can't do. I can't hold something in one hand, unless it's attached with a pin or perhaps tape. And also—I really hate to admit this— there's something else on my "can't do" list. I'll tell you a secret. (*whispers*) I can't kick. (*wails*) You heard me right. *I can't kick*. Really, that's not my fault, though. I have the best excuse in the world. You see, I don't have any legs. The puppeteer's hand fits into my costume right where my legs should be. But that's enough about me. Now I would like you to meet another puppet. (*calls*) Come on out here, Brutus.

BRUTUS: (*enters*) Woof! Woof! Woof!

BRENT: Come over here and let me give you a hug and a pat. . . . Hugs and pats are easy for a hand puppet like me. But I think the boys and girls would like to hear about you now. Let's see, how shall I start?

BRUTUS: Gee, I don't know.

BRENT: Why, that's amazing! You're talking! I never knew that dogs could talk.

BRUTUS: If someone puts words in their mouths, puppet pooches can talk every bit as well as puppet people. But you should know all about that. If someone didn't put words in *your* mouth, you'd be a real dummy for sure.

BRENT:	I'm afraid you're right. And now, since you can talk for yourself, I think I'll toddle offstage and take a rest. Good-bye till later. (*waves and exits*)
BRUTUS:	Well, it's about time I got a chance. Hello, everybody. As Brent told you, my name is Brutus. I am a hand puppet, and, like Brent, I am an actor by profession, because it's my job to appear in puppet plays for kids like you. I can guess what you're thinking. You're thinking that I don't look at all like Brent, and you're right. I don't have arms or forelegs that move, but, as you can see, I do have a mouth that moves, and beautifully, too, if I say so myself. This comes in handy if I'm required to yawn, like this . . . or talk, as I'm doing now, or laugh . . . ha-ha-ha-ha-ha-ha-ha . . . or sing. I think I enjoy singing most of all. Maybe I'll sing a song for you later. . . . And even without legs I can move around on the stage just as well as Brent can. See? (*moves about*) . . . Brent and I are both hand puppets, because we fit over the puppeteer's hand like a glove. In fact, some people would call both of us "glove puppets." But, since Brent can move his hands and arms, I think of him as a *hand-action puppet*. And I think of myself as a *mouth-action puppet*. Well, now that you have learned all about Brent and me, I'd like to have some fun. (*calls*) Brent! Brent! Come out here.
BRENT:	(*enters*) You yelled?
BRUTUS:	Yes, I just had an inspiration.
BRENT:	And what might that be?
BRUTUS:	Let me whisper it to you. (*whispers in Brent's ear*)
BRENT:	(*nodding as he listens*) Yes. . . . I see. . . . Uh-huh. . . . Wonderful idea! Tell the audience about it.
BRUTUS:	Okay. Kids, since Brent likes my idea, I think . . . we wonder . . . uh-uh-uh . . . well, actually I guess we have an announcement.

BRENT: Actually it's kind of an invitation.

BRUTUS: Yes, and it's also . . . uh-uh-uh . . . kind of a question. I was thinking that maybe you kids might enjoy learning some puppet moves. Do you think you'd like that? . . .

BRENT: Hey, wait a minute, Brutus. Before we decide anything, we'd better go backstage and talk to the puppeteers. Without their help, we can't do anything.

BRUTUS: You're right about that. Maybe we could arrange for a spot of music, too. I think music always helps to get folks into the right mood.

BRENT: Another fine idea, Brutus. Let's go see what we can do. Good-bye for now, kids. (*waves and exits*)

BRUTUS: Don't go away. We'll be right back. (*exits*)

* * * * * * * *

(*There should be a brief musical interlude before Act 2. There are two versions of this concluding act. Since the children in the audience are invited to participate, their age should be considered before deciding which version of Act 2 to use.*)

ACT 2

(CONCLUSION 1: PRESCHOOL TO KINDERGARTEN)

(Brent and Brutus enter and stand at center stage)

BRENT: Ok, kids, we're back. Now it's time to have some fun. It was your idea, Brutus, so you do the talking.

BRUTUS: I'll do the talking, Brent, if you do the action. . . . All right, everyone, stand up. . . . Space yourselves on the floor. . . . Don't stand too close together. . . . This won't work if you're all in a bunch. . . . Are you all facing front? . . . Can everyone see us? . . . That's good. Now, I want you to listen to what I say, but keep your eyes on Brent. See if you can do everything that he does. . . . Are you ready? . . . All right! *(shouts)* Let's . . . be . . . puppets! . . . *(Brutus moves to one side leaving Brent at center stage to demonstrate moves as described)* Kids, Brent already showed you some of the things he can do . . . how he can creep and run and skip. Now he will jog in place. Come on, kids, you jog in place too. . . . Jog . . . jog . . . jog . . . jog. . . . Oh, I like the way you're moving. Keep going. . . . Jog . . . jog . . . jog . . . jog. . . . Go faster now, just like Brent. . . . Jog, jog, jog, jog, jog, jog, jog, jog, jog. *(shouts)* That's enough! Stop! . . . Stop! . . . Are you ready to do something else? Maybe something quiet?

BRENT: *(nods)* Yes, let's do something quiet.

BRUTUS: Kids, did you see Brent nod? Show them again, Brent. Keep nodding. . . . That's right. . . . You

199

keep nodding, too, kids. Remember, you're being puppets. Oh, I love to watch you all nodding like that way. It makes you look so agreeable! Nodding always means yes. That goes for puppets and people, too. Now, let's pretend that there is a heavy rock in front of you. Brent, can you see the rock?

BRENT: No. . . . Oh, I mean yes. I forgot it was a pretend rock.

BRUTUS: Well, Brent, I want you to bend over and pick up that rock. Kids, you do what Brent does. Bend down. . . . Put your hands on that pretend rock, and remember that it's very, very heavy. Now, lift. . . . Slowly . . . slowly . . . Lift! Good! You've done it. You're standing up. Brent, is the rock heavy?

BRENT: You better believe it.

BRUTUS: All right, you may put it down. Watch Brent put the rock down, kids, and you do it, too. Be careful, though. Remember, it's heavy. . . . Good! I'm glad you didn't drop those rocks. Now, are you ready for something different? I bet that Brent is. Right, Brent?

BRENT: Right!

BRUTUS: I'm pleased to see you all looking so happy. I think you all should jump for joy. You start the jumping, Brent. . . . Come on, kids, jump for joy. . . . Remember, you're happy again. . . . Jumping is fun, isn't it? I think Brent is jumping more slowly. . . . Are you getting tired again, Brent?

BRENT: Yes, I'm ready to stop. (*collapses*)

BRUTUS: Okay, stop, everybody. It's time to sit down and take a rest. That's right. Sit down on the floor facing the puppet stage. Are you comfortable? . . . Can you see Brent and me all right? . . . Good! I want to tell you kids something. You have been marvelous puppets. I mean it. You have done everything just as well as Brent. . . . Stupendously, I'd say.

BRENT: I agree. In fact, I'd like to give them a big hand. Clapping is something I'm really good at. Kids, give yourselves a hand. (*claps*)

BRUTUS: Yes, clap for yourselves. You deserve it. . . .

BRENT: Now, I have one more thing to do before I leave.

BRUTUS: What's that?

BRENT: I just want to wave good-bye to this beautiful audience. (*waves*) Please wave back to me, kids. . . .

BRUTUS: Waving is fine, and I think you do it as well or better than anything else. But please don't leave yet.

BRENT: Why not? I think this audience knows all about me and the kind of things I can do.

BRUTUS: I think so, too, but aren't you forgetting something?

BRENT: Forgetting something? No, I don't think so.

BRUTUS: Shame on you! I thought you were my friend.

BRENT: I *am* your friend.

BRUTUS: I thought you were my *good* friend.

BRENT: I *am* your *good* friend. I don't know what you're talking about.

BRUTUS: Good friends are supposed to help each other. Didn't I help you show the audience all of your special moves?

BRENT: Yes, you sure did. . . . Oh, dear me! I forgot to thank you. You were a great help, and I do thank you. Now will you forgive me?

BRUTUS: Of course, but since I helped you, now I hope you'll help me.

BRENT: I'd be glad to. But how?

BRUTUS: Well, with the help of my movable mouth, you demonstrated your skills. Now I'd like to show the audience what I can do, and that is sing.

BRENT: What can I do to help?

BRUTUS: You can dance a bit while I sing.

BRENT: It's the least I can do. Are you ready to start?

BRUTUS: I sure am. And, kids, if you know the words, join in. You've been hand-action puppets with Brent. Now you can be mouth-action puppets with me. . . . (*sings while Brent sways to music and claps*)

BRENT: (*clapping hard*) That was really great, Brutus. I'm sure everyone enjoyed it. Is the show over now?

BRUTUS: I can't think of anything more to do. Can you?

BRENT: No, I think we've covered everything.

BRUTUS: In that case, that's all for today. Thanks, kids, and good-bye. (*exits*)

BRENT: I hope we'll meet again sometime. (*bows and exits . . . returns to wave once more*)

ACT 2

(Foam balls, if used for heads, should be passed out at this point. Each child should insert the forefinger of his/her preferred hand into the preformed cavity. . . . Brent and Brutus enter and stand at center stage.)

BRENT: Okay, kids, we're back. Now it's time to have some fun. It was your idea, Brutus, so you do the talking.

BRUTUS: I'll do the talking, Brent, if you do the action.

BRENT: I'd be delighted. Just let me know when to make my moves.

BRUTUS: Will do. Girls and boys, a while ago we showed you some special moves, certain things that hand puppets like Brent and me can do. And now we're about to let you in on some secrets concerning those moves. . . . But before we do that, I'd like to say something about the sound that goes along with the action.

BRENT: Like special sound effects and music?

BRUTUS: I was thinking more about voices. What we say onstage is just as important as the way we move. And real people have to put words into our mouths, or we would be dumb. That's D-U-M-B, dumb. . . .

BRENT: . . . which means that we couldn't speak. And what is a play without speeches?

203

BRUTUS: That would be pantomime. But that's another story.

BRENT: If someone didn't put words in *your* mouth, you couldn't sing either.

BRUTUS: And what a loss to the world of theater that would be!

BRENT: But what about the action? When are we going to get to the good stuff?

BRUTUS: I'm getting to the good stuff now. Besides giving us voices, people behind the scenes have to manipulate us puppets, or we would just stand there like posts.

BRENT: Or, worse yet, lie there like rugs. (*lies down briefly to demonstrate*)

BRUTUS: The people who work the puppets are called puppeteers. It's the puppeteers' secrets that we're about to share with you. So, now at last it's time to have some fun. (*shouts*) Let's . . . be . . . puppets! . . . (*Brutus moves to one side leaving Brent at center stage to demonstrate moves as described*) Can everyone see us? . . . That's good. . . . I want you to listen to what I have to say, but keep your eyes on Brent. . . . Now, I want all of you right-handed people to hold up your right hands. . . . Are there any lefties in the audience? If so, you can use your left hand instead. . . . Pretend that this hand is inside a hand-action puppet like Brent. . . . Your forefinger—that's the one you use for pointing—will be for your puppet's head. That's the finger that a puppeteer would insert into the head of any hand-action puppet. . . . Right next to your forefinger are your thumb on one side . . . and your middle finger—that's the long one—on the other side. These will be your puppet's arms. . . . What? I can guess what you're thinking. You have two fingers left over. What do you use those fingers for? The answer is easy. Nothing. You just tuck

	those fingers into the palm of your hand and forget about them. . . . How am I doing so far, Brent?
BRENT:	Fine. But when do we get to the moves?
BRUTUS:	Right now. Does that make you happy?
BRENT:	Yep. (*nods*)
BRUTUS:	Kids, did you see Brent nod? Show them again, Brent. . . . Keep nodding. . . . That's right. . . . Kids, make your puppet's head nod. Remember to use your forefinger. Keep going. Oh, I love to see all of those nodding fingers. It makes you look so agreeable! Nodding always means yes. That goes for puppets and people, too. . . .
BRENT:	This is getting boring. I'd like to do something else.
BRUTUS:	All right. Pretend you've just seen a puppet play, and you really enjoyed it. What do you do at the end?
BRENT:	I clap, of course, like this. (*claps*)
BRUTUS:	Keep going, Brent. Girls and boys, make your puppet fingers clap, too. Use your thumb and that long middle finger. Tap them together. Keep going. . . . Good!. . . You can also clap in time to music or when your puppet is supposed to be very happy. . . . Ah, Brent seems to be slowing down.
BRENT:	That's enough clapping—until the end of this program, of course. (*laughs*)
BRUTUS:	I seem to remember that you enjoy waving.
BRENT:	Yes, indeed. I love to wave. It's one of the things I do best. (*waves*)
BRUTUS:	Wave back at Brent, kids. Wiggle that long middle finger. . . . Excellent! What else can you do well, Brent?

BRENT: Since I have hands, I can hold props and carry them around the stage. To do that I must use both hands. Pretend with me now. . . . There is a heavy rock in front of your puppet hand. Bend your wrist down, down, down. . . . Using your thumb and middle finger, pick up that make-believe rock, and remember that it is very, very heavy. Now, lift slowly, slowly, slowly. . . . Good! You've done it. You're standing up. Now let's put it down again, slowly, slowly. Don't drop it. Good!

BRUTUS: What about big moves? Puppeteers use their arms more than their hands for some things. Show the kids.

BRENT: Okay. Kids, use those arms to move along with me.

BRUTUS: There's walking. (*Brent moves to side stage and back*) . . .There's running. (*Brent jogs in place*) . . . And there's jumping for joy. (*Brent jumps several times*) . . . Is that about everything?

BRENT: I sure hope so, because I'm tired. Why don't you talk about yourself for a while?

BRUTUS: Talk is a key word here. Since I am a mouth-action puppet, talking is what I'm called upon to do most. Then there's singing and laughing and yawning, all things that require me to open my mouth very wide, like this. . . . But now to get on with the instructions. Most of you kids have used your right hand to practice Brent's moves. Use the other hand to practice mine. First, hold your arm up in front of you with your elbow bent. Next, bend your wrist down, keeping your four fingers straight and pressed tightly together. They will be the top of your puppet's head and upper jaw. Your thumb will be your puppet's lower jaw. When a mouth-action puppet like me is called upon to talk, the puppeteer must open and close these jaws, like this. . . . It's harder than you might think, because the mouth must move to fit the words. Watch while I sing, and move those puppet jaws along with mine. (*sings unaccompanied*)

On top of spaghetti, all covered with cheese,
I lost my poor meatball, when somebody sneezed.
It rolled off the table and onto the floor,
And then my poor meatball rolled out of the door.

BRENT: Bravo! Bravo!

BRUTUS: Thank you very much. You can see, boys and girls, that if your puppet play features an opera singer, a mouth-action puppet like me might get the part.

BRENT: If the opera singer happens to be a dog.

BRUTUS: Now, wait just a minute. People puppets can be mouth-action, and animal puppets can be hand-action. It all depends on what the character has to do in the play.

BRENT: I can think of something else you can do.

BRUTUS: What's that?

BRENT: You can carry props in your mouth.

BRUTUS: Right! And in that event I'd better be an animal. People, even puppet people, don't usually carry things around in their mouths.

BRENT: I've thought of something else *I* can do. And since you kids know our secrets, hold up both hands and move along with the action.

BRUTUS: Both hands? Am *I* in this, too?

BRENT: Yes, but *you* can just stand there. *I* can pat a nice dog on the head, like this. (*pats Brutus*)

BRUTUS: Then *I* can laugh, because that makes me happy. (*laughs*)

BRENT: And I guess *I* can give a hug to a good friend. (*hugs Brutus*)

BRUTUS: That means *I* can lick a good friend's face. (*licks Brent's face*) Well, it's your turn.

BRENT: I'm finished, except for taking a bow. (*bows*)

BRUTUS: You kids can take a bow, too. Thanks for being puppets along with us. You've been great! (*bows head and exits*)

BRENT: Thanks for me, too. Good-bye, everyone. (*exits waving*)

Let's Be Puppets

Production notes

PUPPETS:

Since the play is about hand puppets and their manipulation, the two characters must be as the script describes them. Brent is designated a hand-action puppet and Brutus a mouth-action puppet. If foam balls are used as heads during audience participation in Act 2, it would be fitting if Brent had a similar-type head. The dog puppet should have a mouth that opens very wide.

PROPS:

If the approximate size of the audience can be anticipated, passing out foam balls to use for puppet heads would be appropriate and fun for the children. Each must have a hole gouged out for the child's forefinger. This audience participation segment can proceed without these props, however, since there is no mention of them in the script.

TAPING:

The two characters' voices should be strikingly different. Brutus's voice should be deeper, and he should speak slowly. No special sound effects are needed during the action, but Brutus sings during Act 2, Conclusion 1, so a humorous song must be included. The person recording Brutus's role could do the singing. If a record or cassette is used, the voice should be similar to the speaking voice. When Brutus sings in Act 2, Conclusion 2, it is merely a few lines of "On Top of Spaghetti," so it is worked unaccompanied into the dialogue. Pauses, especially those during the audience participation segments, must be long enough to allow the children to respond to directions.

ACTION: The stage business is easily managed and is described in either the written directions or in the dialogue itself. One puppeteer plays each part, and either may operate the tape player. Except for Brent's brief departure during Brutus's Act 1 monologue, once onstage the puppets remain. They should enter from opposite sides and exit the same way at the end of each act. Act 2, Conclusion 1, which is for younger children, can proceed right after the musical interlude. If foam "heads" are to be used by the audience in Conclusion 2, a longer break will be necessary between acts. Both versions of Act 2 will work more smoothly if an assistant familiar with the action stands in audience view at the side of the puppet stage. This helper can urge the audience to participate according to the timing of the tape and also demonstrate the moves described in the script.

TIME: Act 1, 7 $\frac{1}{2}$ minutes. Act 2, Conclusion 1, 8 minutes. Act 2, Conclusion 2, 10 minutes. Extra time should be allowed for introductory music, interlude, and Brutus's song in Act 2, Conclusion 1.

A VISIT TO THE LIBRARY

CHARACTERS

BOY
GIRL
OLD LADY
CHILDREN'S LIBRARIAN

PROPS

2 BOOKS

(*Boy and Girl enter and look around*)

BOY: This is the library I told you about.

GIRL: (*looks around*) Wow! Look at all the books. There must be millions of them.

BOY: Thousands anyway. And today I'm going to take some of them home with me.

GIRL: Oh, will they let you do that?

BOY: Sure. Anyone with a library card can borrow books.

GIRL: Do you have to have a library card to get books?

BOY: Yes. My father brought me here last week. We filled out an application, and now I have my own card, so today I can take some books home with me.

GIRL: (*loudly*) Oh, I really love books. I'd like to get a library card, too.

OLD LADY: (*enters*) Shhh. . . . Shhh. . . . Hush up, you two.

BOY: Wh-wh-what did we do?

OLD LADY: You were talking much too loudly. This is a library. Don't you children know that you're supposed to whisper in a library?

BOY:	No, we didn't know that.
OLD LADY:	Well, you know it now. A library should be a quiet place, so if you want to talk, go outside. That's all I have to say. (*exits*)
GIRL:	Oh, dear, I guess we should go home.
BOY:	I came here to get some books. I don't want to leave yet.
GIRL:	But that lady works here. She's the library lady.
BOY:	The library lady? Why do you think that?
GIRL:	You can tell by looking at her. She has gray hair pulled back into a little bun at the back. Everyone knows that all library ladies have buns like that . . . and glasses, too.
BOY:	I guess you're right.
GIRL:	I don't want to stay at this library any longer. I don't like a place where I can't even talk.
BOY:	But I want to get some books.
GIRL:	That library lady doesn't like us. I'm going home, and I'm not coming back here anymore.
CH. LIBR:	(*enters*) Hi, kids. How are you today?
BOY:	All right . . . I guess.
CH. LIBR:	Are you looking for some books, something special perhaps?
BOY:	No, I don't think so. I came here to get a couple of books today, but I changed my mind.
CH. LIBR:	I'm so sorry. What happened?
GIRL:	The library lady doesn't like us. She told us to stop talking and go outside.
CH. LIBR:	What library lady? I'm the children's librarian here.
GIRL:	You are?

CH. LIBR:	Why, yes. See, I'm even wearing my special T-shirt today.
GIRL:	(*reads*) It says, I *heart* children's books.
CH. LIBR:	(*laughs*) I can tell you're a good reader. But the heart means *love*, so my T-shirt really says, I *love* children's books.
BOY:	Who was that other lady then?
CH. LIBR:	My goodness, I really don't know.
GIRL:	She was an old lady like my great-grandma, and she had gray hair. It was pulled back into a little bun in back and . . .
CH. LIBR:	(*laughs*) Excuse me for laughing, but, believe me, most women who work in libraries today don't wear their hair pulled back in buns. That lady must have been one of our patrons.
BOY:	What's a patron?
CH. LIBR:	A patron is someone who comes to the library. Doctors have patients, and stores have customers, but the people who use the library are called patrons.
BOY:	So if I borrow a book today, I'll be a patron.
CH. LIBR:	Yes, you will.
GIRL:	What about talking? Are we allowed to talk, or do we have to whisper like that mean lady said?
CH. LIBR:	You don't need to whisper, but please don't be so hard on that lady. When she was a little girl, libraries were quiet places, and everyone whispered. There weren't so many books for children in those days, so fewer kids visited libraries. Today we have thousands of books for people your age, and a good number of our patrons are children.
GIRL:	(*loudly*) And now we kids can talk as loud as we want. Hooray!

CH. LIBR:	Hold it! Hold it! I didn't say that. . . . Some people come here to do homework and study. If you talk in a normal voice, you won't disturb them. But we can't have too much noise. . . . So, no shouting or screaming, and no running or jumping. . . .
BOY:	And no climbing up those shelves either, I'll bet.
CH. LIBR:	Don't even think about it, because then *I* would have to send you outside, and I'd hate to do that.
GIRL:	We'll be good. I'm sure glad you're the library lady here, 'cause you're young and pretty.
CH. LIBR:	Well, thank you. But, listen, you should think of me as the children's librarian, not the library lady.
GIRL:	But, why?
CH. LIBR:	Because some people who have my kind of job are men.
BOY:	Really?
CH. LIBR:	Yes. And children's librarians can be all different ages, shapes, sizes, and races, too! But we are all alike in one way.
GIRL:	What's that?
CH. LIBR:	We all love children and books.
GIRL:	Oh, I see.
CH. LIBR:	That's why being a children's librarian is the perfect job for me. . . . (*addresses boy*) Now, I believe you came here to borrow some books. Let's go over to the children's section and find something you would enjoy. (*all exit*.) . . .
BOY:	(*enters carrying books*) These books look good. I know I'm going to enjoy them.
GIRL:	(*enters*) You sure picked them out in a hurry.

BOY:	I found exactly what I wanted right away. Now I'm going to take them home.
GIRL:	But I wanted to look around for a while.
BOY:	We can come back later. Let's go to the front desk, and while I check these out, you can get an application for a library card.
GIRL:	I'll do that, because I want to borrow books, too.
BOY:	Okay, let's go. (*exits*)
GIRL:	I'm coming. (*looks around*) I really like this library. You'd better believe I'll be back soon . . . and often, too. (*exits*)

A Visit to the Library

Production notes

PUPPETS:	All of the puppets should be hand-action. The old lady must have gray hair in a bun and glasses as described in the script, and the costume for the children's librarian must be inscribed "I ♥ children's books."
SETTING:	All of the action takes place in the central section of a library. The children's area, briefly visited by the boy and girl, is offstage to one side, while the circulation desk is offstage to the opposite side. No prop stage is needed.
PROPS:	The only props are the two books that the boy borrows. They should be small picture books, the lightest weight possible.
TAPING:	No special sound effects are needed. The boy and girl should have childlike voices, each with a different pitch that is maintained throughout. The old lady's voice should sound querulous, and the voice of the children's librarian should be sweet and soothing.
ACTION:	The puppeteer on the right should be the boy and the girl. The puppeteer on the left should be the other two characters and operate the tape player. The boy and girl first enter from the right and stay at center stage until briefly exiting and reentering at the left. Their final exit is to the right. Both the old lady and the children's librarian enter from the left and exit the same way.
TIME:	7 minutes.

SPRING THINGS

PUPPETS	PROP
BOY GIRL	KITE

(Boy and girl enter from opposite sides and move to center stage facing audience)

BOY:
Spring things, spring things,
Now's the time for spring things.

GIRL:
I certainly agree with you about that. It's a lovely spring day. Do you have any particular things in mind?

BOY:
It's time to put away the sled,
Time to get your bike instead.

GIRL:
What a terrific idea! But, poor me, I don't have a bike.

BOY:
Then put away your winter hat.
Find your baseball cap and bat.

GIRL:
That's another good springtime suggestion, but I don't have either of those items either. Do you have any other ideas?

BOY:
Ice skates? Skis? Pack them away.
Get out your roller skates today.

GIRL:
Ah, at last you've mentioned something that I happen to own. I was beginning to feel pretty

sorry for myself. But I can't remember where I put my roller skates. Maybe they're in the basement, but I'm not sure. I'd have to look and look and look, and that might take a long time, so I hope you can think of something else.

BOY: Spring things, spring things,
Now's the time for spring things.

GIRL: Your little poems are beginning to irritate me. Do you always have to speak in verse?

BOY: No, I don't have to. I was just practicing a bit of bouncy rhyme talk. . . . It's fun.

GIRL: Be serious for a minute. Do you have any practical suggestions about what we can do?

BOY: Actually yes. . . .

Since the day is clear and bright,
How'd you like to fly a kite?

GIRL: Hey, you said you didn't have to talk in rhyme.

BOY: I'm sorry. I just couldn't help myself. Flying a kite seems so springlike, and it's the last thing I can think of.

GIRL: But, guess what—and I really hate to say it again—I don't own a kite.

BOY: That doesn't matter. I have a new kite at home, and you can help me fly it. Wait here and I'll get it. (*exits*)

GIRL: At last he came up with something I can do, too. And I have to admit that flying a kite is a perfect spring thing.

BOY: (*enters with kite*) The wind is kicking up a bit. This is going to be fun.

GIRL: How do we do it?

BOY:	Just watch. My dad showed me how. I stand with my back to the wind like this. (*turns*) Then I lift the kite and let the wind do the work. (*lifts kite*) Fly, kite, fly. . . . (*kite rises*) Wheeee! . . . There it goes!
GIRL:	(*looking up*) Ooooooh! . . . It's really flying.
BOY:	This may be the best spring thing of all. Kites and spring really go together, like eggs and ham.
GIRL:	Yes, they do. Now, when do I get my turn?
BOY:	You'll have to wait. I don't want it to get caught in that tree. Everyone knows that trees can eat kites.
GIRL:	Hey, I want my turn. You promised.
BOY:	All right. All right. In a minute. . . . (*sound of thunder*) . . . Oh, no! It's going to rain. I'll have to bring the kite down.
GIRL:	Hurry! The kite shouldn't get wet.
BOY:	I'm not supposed to do it too fast. I'm glad it's not very high in the sky.
GIRL:	I feel some raindrops. Can't you hurry a little bit?
BOY:	Ah, here it comes. (*kite flutters down and boy picks it up*) Now we'll have to run for it. Let's duck inside that building over there. . . . (*sound of thunder . . . they exit on one side and immediately enter opposite.*) . . . Hey, this is the library! Oh, man, look at all the books!
GIRL:	You sound surprised. Didn't you know we came in the back door of the library? Haven't you been here before?
BOY:	No, this is my very first time. Have you been here before?
GIRL:	Sure, I come here all the time, and now I'm the one to have an idea. Why don't we read a book today?

BOY: You mean read it here?

GIRL: Yes. Can you think of a better thing to do while we wait out this spring shower?

BOY: No, I guess not.

GIRL: I'm glad I finally came up with the best idea for today. And think about it. Rain is a spring thing, so reading a book on a rainy day can be a spring thing, too. . . . The children's room is over there. (*points*) They have all kinds of books for kids. Later, when the rain stops, we can take the kite outside again, and then it will be *my* turn to fly it. . . . Meanwhile, let's go look at the books.

BOY: All right.

GIRL: Come on. What are you waiting for?

BOY: I just can't help myself. I was trying to think of a rhyme.

GIRL: Oh, no. Not again.

BOY: Wait a second. . . . Yes, I've got it.

Spring things, spring things,
Now's the time for spring things.
Especially when it rains, it's true,
A book can be a spring thing, too.

Spring Things

PUPPETS: Both puppets should be hand-action, dressed to indicate that one is a boy and the other a girl.

SETTING: The change of scene from outdoors to inside the library is managed by both puppets exiting in one direction and reentering from the other. No prop stage is needed.

PROPS: The kite, the only prop, should be made of paper reinforced by gluing on toothpicks, crisscross and at the edges. It should be diamond-shaped and have a tail with a few bows. The string that the boy holds should be white and attached to the middle of the kite. Heavy black thread attached to the top will allow a puppeteer to lift it from above.

TAPING: The only sound effect is the thunder. While a foil pan could be used, pressing and shaking an aluminum cookie sheet makes a lower sound and more convincing thunder. The characters' voices should be noticeably different. Sufficient time should be allowed for the boy to get his kite and also for the characters to exit one way and reenter from the opposite side.

ACTION: With only two characters, the action would be very simple, if the kite did not have to be lifted from above. Since one puppeteer must be standing to do this, the other must manipulate both puppets. The puppeteer on the left can assume this job and should wear the boy puppet on his/her left

221

hand and the girl on the right hand. Then the boy can easily enter from the left and the girl from the right. The boy exits left to get the kite. Before the show, the black lifting thread should be taped onto the inside of the backdrop's curtain rod, well out of audience view behind the side curtain. It will be the job of the puppeteer on the right to see that the boy is holding the kite properly and then to remove the tape holding the black thread. This thread must be firmly held and gently manipulated until the script calls for the kite to flutter down. Then the black thread is dropped. The boy puppet, meanwhile, should be touching the kite string, as if in control of the kite. These moves should be practiced until they go smoothly. Once the boy has the kite back in hand, both puppets should quickly exit to the right and immediately reenter from the left to indicate the change of scene from outdoors to the library. The puppeteer on the right should operate the tape player.

TIME: 6 $1/2$ minutes.

SUN FUN

CHARACTERS

BOY
GIRL

PROPS

LIBRARY CARD
2 BOOKS

(*Boy and Girl enter from opposite sides and move to center stage facing audience*)

BOY: Sun fun, sun fun,
Now's the time for sun fun.

GIRL: Summer's here. It's time to play.
What is there to do today?

BOY: Hey, I know what to do today.

GIRL: What?

BOY: Let's go swimming.

GIRL: Fine idea! Do you know how to swim?

BOY: Sure. You just jump into the water like this (*jumps*) and kick your legs and paddle your arms like this. (*paddles arms*)

GIRL: (*laughs*) That's a good joke. I can tell that you don't know how to swim. Well, I don't know how to swim either. Maybe we should think of something else.

BOY: Sun fun, sun fun,
Now's the time for sun fun.

GIRL: Summer's here. It's time to play.
What is there to do today?

BOY:	Hey, I know what to do today.
GIRL:	What?
BOY:	Let's play baseball.
GIRL:	Excellent idea! Baseball is an all-time great summer game. All you need are a ball and a bat . . .
BOY:	And nine kids on each team.
GIRL:	Oops! That'll be a problem. We don't know that many kids.
BOY:	Sure we do. Our school is full of kids.
GIRL:	But school's out now.
BOY:	Oh, that's right. It's summer vacation.
GIRL:	And you know what that means.
BOY:	Yeah! No teachers and no lessons.
GIRL:	And no kids for baseball teams.
BOY:	Sun fun, sun fun, Now's the time for sun fun.
GIRL:	Yes, summer's here. It's time to play. What is there to do today?
BOY:	Well, we could play baseball by ourselves. You could pitch the ball (*simulates pitch*) and I could bat. (*simulates batting*) . . .
GIRL:	Or better yet, *you* could pitch the ball (*simulates pitch*) and *I* could bat. (*simulates batting*) . . . Boom! Right out of the park!
BOY:	Okay, I'll pitch. Go get your ball and bat.
GIRL:	I don't have a ball and bat. I thought you did.
BOY:	Nope.
GIRL:	Well, that's out.
BOY:	Sun fun, sun fun. Now's the time for sun fun.

GIRL: Summer's here. It's time to play.
What is there to do today?

BOY: I hear fishing is fun.

GIRL: Fishing? Superb idea! But I don't have a fishing pole. Do you?

BOY: No, but we could use a stick and a piece of string for a line.

GIRL: And a bent pin for a hook.

BOY: Then we go down to the river and fish.

GIRL: Uh-oh, I just thought of something.

BOY: What?

GIRL: The river's on the other side of Main Street, and my mother won't let me cross Main Street.

BOY: Mine either.

GIRL: Well, we're right back where we started.

BOY: Sun fun, sun fun,
Now's the time for sun fun.

GIRL: Summer's here. It's time to play,
And *I* know what to do today!

BOY: Do you really have an idea?

GIRL: (*dancing happily*) Yes, yes, yes. You wait here. I'll be right back. . . . (*exits and reenters with a library card*)

BOY: What's that?

GIRL: It's my library card.

BOY: Don't tell me you want to go to the library.

GIRL: Yes, I do, and it's the best idea we've come up with yet.

BOY: But it's summer vacation. Don't you remember "Sun fun, sun fun?" We want to do something special.

GIRL: Yes, and that's why we should go to the library. There will be lots of special programs this summer. There's story time and movies and crafts—all sorts of things—and there's also a summer reading club!

BOY: You're right! I've heard about that.

GIRL: Well, what are we waiting for? Let's go. (*both exit and reenter immediately, each carrying a book*)

BOY: Sun fun, sun fun,
Now's the time for sun fun.

GIRL: Summer's here, and we will play
And also read a book today!

Sun Fun

Production notes

PUPPETS:
Both characters should be hand-action puppets since they are required to make arm motions and carry books. Although one is a boy and the other a girl, they should be compatible in size and appearance.

PROPS:
Even if this show is not presented in a library, the library card should be "official," since many children in the audience will know what a real one looks like. The books that the puppets are required to carry briefly should be picture books familiar to the audience and small enough to be held easily.

TAPING:
This skit is entirely dialogue. Even though the puppets are supposed to be children, the boy's could be an adult male voice. If it is not too deep, the audience will accept it as belonging to a boy. This difference will make the puppeteers' job much easier. The general tone of the conversation is upbeat, and the cadence of the rhyme should be swingy.

ACTION:
In a pinch the action, which is about as simple as a puppet play can be, could be managed by one person. Since, presumably, the program would include other plays that would require two puppeteers, the roles in this one might as well be assigned to different people. The puppets first enter from opposite sides—it doesn't matter which—and the girl exits on her entry side to get

her library card. Both can then exit and reenter with their books on the boy's side. They should use the motions that the script suggests and stand very still when not speaking. While "rapping," they should sway rhythmically from side to side. The tape player may be operated by either puppeteer.

TIME: 5 $1/2$ minutes.

JEREMY BORROWS A BOOK

CHARACTERS

NARRATOR
JEREMY
MRS. HILL
BITSY
SNOOKIE
PUPPY

PROPS

LIBRARY BOOK
CRAYON

JEREMY: *(sings offstage)*

Here, here, here I come from the li-brar-ee.
Merrily, merrily, merrily, merrily, with a book
    for me.

NARRATOR: Somebody's happy today. Here he comes, skipping around the corner now, and he's carrying something. Ah, yes. It's Jeremy Johnson, and that's a book he has.

JEREMY: *(enters with book)* I'm home. . . . I'm home. . . .

MRS. HILL: *(enters)* Well, Jeremy, it's about time. You know you're supposed to come right home after school.

JEREMY: But, Mrs. Hill . . .

MRS. HILL: No "buts," please. I was really worried about you. Why, I was just about to call the police.

JEREMY: But, Mrs. Hill . . .

MRS. HILL: I don't have time to go looking for you, Jeremy. You must remember that I am very busy taking care of Bitsy and Snookie all day, not to mention your new puppy. Why, I must be the busiest

229

	baby-sitter in town, as well as the best—at least, that's what your parents tell me. But, never mind about that. It's my job to be the baby-sitter, and it's your job to come right home after school.
JEREMY:	I know that, Mrs. Hill, but . . .
MRS. HILL:	Where were you, Jeremy? And your answer better be good.
JEREMY:	I was at the library.
MRS. HILL:	Oh? . . . Oh! . . . Well, that's a pretty good answer, I guess. But why did you decide to do that today?
JEREMY:	Because I have a new library card, and I wanted to borrow a book to read tonight. See, here it is. (*shows book*) I didn't think you'd get mad at me for stopping at the library, especially since I always pass it on my way home from school.
MRS. HILL:	I'm not mad at you, Jeremy. But next time, please remember to tell me if you're going to be late.
JEREMY:	All right, I will. Does that mean I still get my after-school snack?
MRS. HILL:	Of course. How about oatmeal cookies still warm from the oven?
JEREMY:	Oh, yum! You're the best cookie baker in the world, besides being the best baby-sitter.
MRS. HILL:	(*laughs*) How could I ever be mad at you, Jeremy? Come along with me now. (*exits*)
JEREMY:	I'm coming. (*places book on floor and exits*)
NARRATOR:	So Jeremy goes off to enjoy his snack, leaving his library book on the floor. . . . Now someone else is coming, a very small someone. It's Bitsy, Jeremy's baby sister. Bitsy doesn't walk or talk yet, but she can certainly crawl.
BITSY:	(*enters crawling and making jabbering baby sounds*) . . .

NARRATOR:	(*as Bitsy moves accordingly*) Bitsy sees the book. Surely anything left on the floor must be meant for her. Why else would it be there? But wait. Would a baby be interested in a book? You bet she would. . . . Hey, Bitsy, pick up the book. Now give it a good shake. Aw, it doesn't rattle. That's no fun. But, look. It opens. What's this inside? Paper! Paper is fun for a baby. Remember Daddy's newspaper? You sure made a mess of that. Yes, paper can be crumpled and torn. . . . Bitsy is leafing through the book. What pretty pages it has! Should she crumple them up or tear them out? She's thinking this over. . . .
JEREMY:	(*enters yelling*) Bitsy! Stop!
BITSY:	(*drops book*) Wah! Wa-a-ah! Wa-a-a-a-ah!
JEREMY:	Shame on you, Bitsy. That's my library book, and you were about to tear the pages. I know what you did to Daddy's newspaper yesterday. Well, you're not going to wreck my book. I'm taking you right back to Mrs. Hill. (*picks up Bitsy and exits, Bitsy crying*)
NARRATOR:	That was close, but the library book is safe for the moment. Do you notice that it is still on the floor? Uh-oh, someone else is coming. It's Snookie, Jeremy's little brother.
SNOOKIE:	(*enters with crayon*) Crayon. . . . Pretty crayon. . . . Snookie draw.
NARRATOR:	(*as Snookie moves accordingly*) Snookie loves to draw. Someday, no doubt, he'll be a great artist. But, of course, he needs to practice his art. He's looking at the wall now, raising his crayon. But, no. He remembers that Mrs. Hill wouldn't like that. Mrs. Hill was very, *very* unhappy the last time he drew on the wall. She scrubbed his pretty picture away, quite fast, before Mother and Daddy came home. Naughty, naughty boy, she said. Walls are not for

drawing. Paper is for drawing. . . .Ah, Snookie sees the library book. He knows that books have stories inside, and he likes to listen to stories read aloud. He also knows that books have pages, paper pages. And paper is for drawing. Mrs. Hill said so. Snookie touches the book. He raises his crayon. . . .

JEREMY: (*enters yelling*) Snookie! Stop! You can't scribble in that book. Give it here.

SNOOKIE: (*falling onto book*) No, no, no. Snookie draw.

JEREMY: You're not supposed to draw on book paper. You use regular paper for drawing.

SNOOKIE: (*crying*) Wanna draw. Wanna draw.

JEREMY: All right. All right. Come with me, and I'll give you some drawing paper. (*Both exit.*)

NARRATOR: Well, that's another close call. Jeremy has saved his book again. But there it is, still on the floor. . . . What possibly could happen next? . . . Aha! I'm afraid I can guess. Jeremy has a puppy, and here she comes now.

PUPPY: (*enters*) Woof! Woof!

NARRATOR: (*as puppy moves accordingly*) The puppy seems to be searching for something. Just look at her, sniffing about, here, there, everywhere. She's probably hoping to find something to chew. Puppies love to chew on almost anything left lying about. Mother's purse, Daddy's shoe or wallet, whatever is handy. There are no shoes or purses handy today. But here's something nice. . . . (*picks up book*)

JEREMY: (*enters*) Aarrggh! That's my library book. (*grabs at book*) Let go. Let go, I say. Bad puppy. Bad, bad, bad! (*puppy and Jeremy tug at book*) Let go. Aarrggh!

MRS. HILL: (*enters*) My goodness, what's going on here?

JEREMY:	The puppy was chewing my library book.
MRS. HILL:	(*taking book*) Let me see. . . . It seems to be all right.
JEREMY:	I saved it just in time again. First Bitsy was about to rip it apart, and then Snookie started to draw in it, and now the puppy wants to eat it. Nothing is safe in this house.
MRS. HILL:	Tell me, Jeremy, where did Bitsy and Snookie and the puppy find this book?
JEREMY:	Right here on the floor where I put it when I . . . Uh-oh.
MRS. HILL:	I think you've just realized that the floor is not the best place to keep a book. Here it is. (*hands book to Jeremy*) Now, what are you going to do with it?
JEREMY:	I'm going to take it upstairs and put it on my dresser.
MRS. HILL:	Good. I'm sure it will be safe there.
JEREMY:	I'll read it tonight, and tomorrow I'll take it back and get another one, maybe two or three, or even more, lots more.
MRS. HILL:	Don't get more than you can carry home. You wouldn't want to lose one.
JEREMY:	Don't worry. After this, I'm going to take care of all the books I borrow. And I'm starting right now. (*exits with book*)
MRS. HILL:	(*calling after him*) You're a good boy, Jeremy. (*exits*)
NARRATOR:	And from now on, Jeremy will be a good library patron, too. When he returns that book, I'm sure it will be the same as it was when he borrowed it. Then, the next time *you* visit the library, perhaps you will see it and want to borrow it, too.

Jeremy Borrows a Book

Production notes

PUPPETS:
Since the puppy holds the book in its mouth, it must be a mouth-action puppet. The others should be hand-action puppets. Puppets with foam ball heads would work well. Smaller balls could be used for Bitsy and Snookie to indicate their young age. Bitsy could be bald with a single (pipe cleaner) hair.

SETTING:
A prop stage is needed for the book.

PROPS:
Jeremy's book should be a reader with a familiar title such as *Green Eggs and Ham*. The crayon should be a color that will contrast with the backdrop.

TAPING:
The introductory song that Jeremy sings offstage is to the tune of "Row, Row, Row Your Boat." There are no special sound effects needed in the play. The recorders' voices should suit the characters they represent, especially with regard to age. The narrator may be any good reader.

ACTION:
The puppeteer on the left should be Jeremy and the puppy. The puppeteer on the right should operate the tape player and take all the other parts in turn. Jeremy's first entrance is from the left. All other entrances and exits should be at the right.

TIME:
8 minutes.

A CLASS VISIT TO THE LIBRARY

CHARACTERS	PROPS
LIBRARIAN ASSISTANT	MONEY BUCKET GLOBE POSTER PICTURE OF FAMOUS PERSON LIBRARY CARD

LIBRARIAN: *(enters)* Hello, everyone. How are you all today? . . . Good! . . . Welcome to my library. This is a very special place. It's a place I hope you'll visit often, because . . . well, I'll talk about that later. . . . Now I have a question to ask. . . . How many of you out there are rich? *(raises hand)* . . .Did I see a teacher's hand go up? . . .Well, did you notice that *I* raised *my* hand? . . .Yes, I am rich. I admit it, and I have a fine assistant who will help me prove my point. *(calls)* Please, would you bring out my money bucket?

ASSISTANT: *(enters with bucket)* Here it is.

LIBRARIAN: Now, please pour out the contents.

ASSISTANT: Okay, if you say so. *(inverts bucket)*

LIBRARIAN: Oh, my goodness! Nothing came out of the bucket. It was empty. *(talks to Assistant)* You might as well take this empty bucket away. *(Assistant exits with bucket.)* . . .All right, so I don't have a bucket of money, but I don't need to be a millionaire to be rich and to do some things that millionaires do. . . . I have traveled far and wide. Just ask my assistant. . . .

ASSISTANT:	(*enters with globe poster*) Yes, indeed, all over the world. (*exits with poster*) . . .
LIBRARIAN:	And I have met all sorts of famous people, some from the long-ago past. . . .
ASSISTANT:	(*enters with picture of famous person*) Here's someone everyone will recognize. (*exits with picture*) . . .
LIBRARIAN:	How did I manage this without having a bucketful of money? . . . I'll tell you a secret. I have a key to a treasure house. That treasure house is this library, and the key that opens the door to the treasure house is my library card. Some of you may already have a library card, so you know what I mean. Now, I have some things to say to those of you who *don't* have one. (*calls*) Assistant, would you please bring my card out here to show the boys and girls?
ASSISTANT:	(*enters with library card*) Here it is, the official card of the Public Library.
LIBRARIAN:	But this particular card belongs to me, and I alone must use it.
ASSISTANT:	Since I'm a friend of yours, would you let me use it, if I left my library card at home?
LIBRARIAN:	Would I let you use my credit card if you left your credit card at home?
ASSISTANT:	No, I'm pretty sure you wouldn't lend me your credit card.
LIBRARIAN:	Well, my library card is just like a credit card. If I let you use it to borrow books, and you forgot to bring those books back, the library would blame me. I want to keep my record clear, so no one else is going to use *this* card.
ASSISTANT:	That's something everyone should remember.
LIBRARIAN:	Now, I would like to introduce someone who is going to tell you how you can get your own library card. I'll be back later.

* * * * * * * *

(The children's librarian or some other well-informed person on the library staff should explain the procedure for obtaining a library card and perhaps dispense application forms. Library rules, open hours, loan periods, types of materials available, etc. should be discussed here and questions answered.)

* * * * * * * *

LIBRARIAN: *(enters)* Now you know all about this special place, this treasure house open to everyone who has a key, this gold mine available to anyone who will dig. . . . A while ago I said that I hope you will visit the library often. I think that going to the library should be included as part of every person's way of life, something that is done regularly. Most people visit the grocery store every week, sometimes more. A trip to the supermarket provides food for the body. Well, a trip to the library provides food for the mind. . . . Maybe you'd like to know how to do magic tricks, how to make a kite, how to cook a Chinese dinner. If so, come to the library. . . . Maybe you'd like to meet Martin Luther King, Princess Diana, or Cleopatra. if so, come to the library. You won't meet them in person, but if you read a biography, you'll feel as if you know them. . . . Maybe you'd like to know more about dinosaurs or trains or space travel. If so, come to the library. . . . And I haven't even mentioned the shelves of picture books, fairy tales, and fiction of all kinds, things you read for the fun of it. You'll find stories of every kind here at the library, this wonderful treasure house that's open to all. . . . I think I've remembered everything I meant to say. *(calls offstage)* Assistant, can you think of anything else?

ASSISTANT: *(enters)* You might mention that the price of admission is right.

LIBRARIAN: Oh, I'm glad you thought of that. Boys and girls, as long as you take good care of the books you borrow and bring them back on time, the library is absolutely free. Not many of the good things in life are free, but the library is. Talk about the price being right! (*turns to Assistant*) Now, I think we've covered everything, haven't we?

ASSISTANT: (*nods*) Yes, I can't think of another thing to add. If the kids have any questions, they can ask someone who works here.

LIBRARIAN: Thank you very much, girls and boys. I've enjoyed talking to you, and I hope to see you back here very soon. (*exits*)

ASSISTANT: And often, too. (*bows and exits waving*)

A CLASS VISIT TO THE LIBRARY

Production notes

PUPPETS: The librarian puppet can be either hand- or mouth-action. The assistant must be hand-action in order to maneuver the props. Since gender is not mentioned, they can be either male or female in appearance.

PROPS: The plastic top from an aerosol spray can will work as a money bucket. The globe poster should be a cardboard disk, painted to resemble the world, and glued to an ice cream stick axis for the assistant to hold. The picture of a famous person should be someone (such as Abraham Lincoln) whom everyone will recognize and should be mounted on cardboard. It, too, can be glued signlike to an ice cream stick. The library card should be an official example.

TAPING: The voices should be male or female in accordance with the puppets used. The librarian should sound older than the assistant. The most important thing to remember is to allow enough time during the pauses for the various props to be brought onstage, displayed briefly, and removed. Since this is a generic piece, suitable for any public library, the script calls for the taping to be interrupted so that specific information can be included in the program. While this could be prerecorded as a puppet speech and incorporated into the play, the appearance of an actual person who can dispense forms, answer questions, etc., is advised, after which the play can continue.

ACTION: One puppeteer (either) should be the librarian, and the other should work the tape player and take the assistant's role. The librarian should stay at center stage and make entrances and exits on the same side that the assistant does. The assistant, who is required to make brief appearances holding different props, should stay to one side. Rather than turning to exit, the puppet can simply back off the stage.

TIME: 6 minutes. Allow extra time for the insertion of specific library information.

BUYING PUPPETS

Puppet manufacturers and/or stores are listed in the yellow pages of many phone books, especially in large market areas. Toy stores often sell puppets or can suggest places where they might be purchased. The following companies responded to a letter with regard to buying manufactured puppets:

ENCHANTED FOREST, 85 Mercer Street, New York, NY 10012. A variety of animal puppets. Order by mail or by phone, toll-free 1-800-456-4449 between 11 A.M. and 7 P.M. Catalog available. Customers are invited to visit the store to be shown around.

FOLKMANIS, INC., 1219 Park Ave., Emeryville, CA 94608. Wholesale catalog available to schools and nonprofit organizations.

HUGGABLE HAND PUPPETS, P.O. Box 98054, Raleigh, NC 27624-8054. Tel. or Fax 919-790-7091. Catalog for 150 animal, character, and fantasy character puppets sent upon request. Most orders shipped within 10 days; special orders may take longer.

MANATEE TOY COMPANY, 131 Beach Ln., Crystal Lane, FL 32629. Has a lovely manatee puppet.

MARY MEYER CORPORATION, Rte. 30, P.O. Box 275, Townshend, VT 05353. Sell wholesale to schools, etc., with a minimum purchase of $50.

MR. ANDERSON'S COMPANY, 301 Nippersink Dr., McHenry, IL 60050. Sell only to schools and public libraries.

NANCY RENFRO STUDIOS, P.O. Box 164226, Austin, TX 78716. Accept MC/VISA phone orders at 1-800-933-5512. Other calls, 512-327-9588. Call or write for free catalog.

PUPPET ON THE PIER, Pier 39, Space H-4, San Francisco, CA 94133. Catalog available. 20% discount to public libraries and schools. Call toll free 1-800-443-4463.

PUPPET SOURCE, Langtry Publications,7838 Burnet Ave., Van Nuys, CA 91405-1051. Orders can be faxed or sent by mail; no phone orders. Sell exclusively to libraries and schools. Orders must be accompanied by a purchase order or written on library stationery and signed by an authorized person. Individual orders must enclose a check or money order. More than 100 holiday, animal, and people puppets available.

SPECIAL EFFECTS, 925 Amboy Ave., Perth Amboy, NJ 08861.

STAR MERCHANDISE COMPANY, INC., P.O. Box 3609, Thousand Oaks, CA 91359. Minimum order $25. No C.O.D.

THE VELVET STABLE, INC., P.O. Box 148, Glastonbury, CT 06033. Inspired by actual living animals and constructed out of the finest materials.

For further information on where to buy puppets, write to: TOY MANU-FACTURERS OF AMERICA, 200 Fifth Ave., New York, NY 10010.

RECOMMENDED READING

Baird, Bil. *The Art of the Puppet*. New York: Macmillan, 1965.

Cole, Nancy H. *Puppet Theater in Performance*. New York: William Morrow and Company, Inc., 1978.

Currell, David. *The Complete Book of Puppet Theatre*. Totowa, New Jersey: Barnes & Noble Books, 1985.

————. *The Complete Book of Puppetry*. Boston: Plays, Inc., 1975.

Engler, Larry and Carol Fijan. *Making Puppets Come Alive*. New York: Taplinger Publishing Co., 1973.

Fijan, Carol and Frank Ballard. *Directing Puppet Theatre*. San Jose, California: Resource Publications, Inc., 1989.

Flower, Cedric and Alan Fortney. *Puppets: Methods and Materials*. Worcester, Massachusetts: Davis Publications, 1983.

Freericks, Mary with Joyce Segal. *Creative Puppetry in the Classroom*. Rowayton, Connecticut: New Plays Books, 1979.

McLaren, Esme. *Making Glove Puppets*. Boston: Plays, Inc., 1973.

MacLenna, Jennifer. *Simple Puppets You Can Make*. New York: Sterling Publishing Co., 1988.

Renfro, Nancy. *A Puppet Corner in Every Library*. Austin, Texas: Nancy Renfro Studios, 1978.

————. *Puppet Shows Made Easy!* Austin, Texas: Nancy Renfro Studios, 1984.

Ross, Laura. *Hand Puppets: How to Make and Use Them*. New York: Lothrop, Lee & Shepard, 1969.
(also in paperback—New York: Dover, 1989)

Roth, Charlene Davis. *The Art of Making Puppets and Marionettes*. Radnor, Pennsylvania: Chilton Book Company, 1975.

Tichenor, Tom. *Tom Tichenor's Puppets*. Nashville, Tennessee: Abingdon Press, 1971.

ABOUT THE AUTHOR

PHYLLIS NOE PFLOMM attended Stephens College and is a graduate of Barnard College. She has worked at specialized and public libraries in New York and is currently a children's librarian in the Dayton & Montgomery County Public Library system in Dayton, Ohio. She is the author of a collection of drawing stories, *Chalk in Hand: The Draw and Tell Book* (Scarecrow Press, 1986).